I AM A
SEAL TEAM SIX
WARRIOR

MEMOIRS OF AN AMERICAN SOLDIER

Howard E. Wasdin
and Stephen Templin

ST. MARTIN'S GRIFFIN

NEW YORK

SOME NAMES, PLACES, TIMES, AND TACTICS
HAVE BEEN CHANGED OR OMITTED TO PROTECT
OPERATORS AND THEIR MISSIONS.

www.stmartins.com

ISBN 978-1-250-01643-0

16   17   18   19   20

CONTENTS

Contents

PART THREE

AUTHOR'S NOTE

For years I was bombarded with questions about my experiences as a U.S. Navy SEAL. People were curious about BUD/S training and my experiences in SEAL Teams Two and Six. My experiences weren't always enjoyable, but they were always adrenaline-filled! This book was originally published for an adult audience; however, I decided that I also wanted to make my story available to young readers, readers like you, so you can understand the sacrifice and dedication of our soldiers as well and hopefully be inspired by the story of a man who overcame so much to achieve his goals. Hopefully as you read about my life, you will understand that there are no limits to what you can achieve in your life, only obstacles to overcome or maneuver around. "The only easy day was yesterday." HOOYAH!

Howard E. Wasdin, Doctor of Chiropractic,
former SEAL Team Six sniper

PART ONE

I like shooting, and I love hunting. But I never did enjoy killing anybody. It's my job. If I don't get those bastards, then they're gonna kill a lot of these kids dressed up like Marines.

—Gunnery Sergeant Carlos Hathcock,
MARINE CORPS SNIPER

Reach Out and Touch Someone

When the U.S. Navy sends their elite, they send the SEALs. When the SEALs send their elite, they send SEAL Team Six. It's the navy's equivalent to the army's Delta Force. Its job is to fight terrorism and armed rebellion, often secretly.

I was a sniper for SEAL Team Six.

This is the first time a SEAL Team Six sniper's story has been told. My story.

In the morning darkness of September 18, 1993, in Mogadishu, Somalia, another SEAL and I crept over a wall and up to the top of a six-story tower. Below us, people were waking up. Men, women, and children relieved themselves in the streets. I smelled the morning fires, fueled by dried animal dung. The fires heated the little food the Somalis had. The warlord who ruled this part of the city, Mohamed Farah Aidid, controlled the population by controlling the food supply. Every time I saw a starving child, I blamed Aidid.

Although the middle of a city may not seem the logical place for navy commandos, SEALs are trained to fight anywhere. That's where the name comes from: SEa, Air and Land. On many operations, we were in all three: We'd parachute in, complete our task on land, and make our way back on water.

From the tower we watched what looked like a large garage

with no roof. It was a vehicle body shop. Surrounding it was a city of despair. Somalis trudged along with their heads and shoulders lowered. Helplessness dimmed their faces, and starvation pulled the skin tight across their bones. This "better" part of town had multilevel, concrete buildings instead of the tin and wooden lean-to sheds that dominated most of the city and countryside. Nevertheless, the smell of human waste and death filled the air.

I played different scenarios over in my mind: one enemy popping out at one location, then another popping up at another location, and so on. I would acquire, aim, and even do a simulated trigger pull, going through my rehearsed breathing and follow-through routine while picturing the actual engagement. Then I simulated reloading and getting back into position looking through my scope, continuing to scan for more "booger-eaters"—the SEAL term for bad guys.

I had done this dry firing and actual firing thousands of times—wet, dry, muddy, snowbound, from a dug-in hole in the ground, from the window of a tall building, and nearly every which way imaginable. The words drilled into our heads since SEAL training were, "The more you sweat in peacetime, the less you bleed in war." This particular day, I was charged with making sure none of my Delta Force buddies sprang a leak as I covered their insertion into the garage. That was every bit as important as my not bleeding.

Our target for this mission was Osman Ali Atto—warlord Aidid's main financier. Atto and his boss had killed hundreds of thousands of Somalis. I felt that if we could kill Atto and Aidid, we could stop the fighting, get the food to the people quickly, and go home in one piece. But the goal of this mission was just to capture Atto, not kill him.

Around 0815 our "asset"—our informer—gave the predetermined signal that Atto was there. My SEAL teammate and I launched the "full package." Little Bird and Black Hawk helicopters filled the sky.

Delta Force operators fast-roped into the roofless garage, dropping lines from the helicopter and sliding right to the ground. Rangers fast-roped around the outside of it. Little Birds flew overhead with Delta snipers to protect the assault force.

Atto's people scattered like rats. Enemy militia shot at the helicopters.

In this environment, an enemy could appear from anywhere, dressed the same as a civilian. Even if he appeared with a gun, there was a chance he was part of a clan on our side. We had to wait until the person pointed the weapon at us. Then we would ensure the enemy ceased to exist. There was no time for makeup or second shots.

Like my SEAL teammate—his nickname was Casanova—I wielded .300 Win Mag sniper rifle. Through my scope, I saw a militiaman 500 yards away firing through an open window at the helos. I made a mental note to keep my heart rate down and centered the crosshairs on him as my muscle memory took over— stock firmly into the shoulder, cheek positioned behind the scope, eye focused on the center of the crosshairs rather than the enemy, and steady trigger squeezing. I felt the gratifying recoil of my rifle. The round hit him in the side of the chest. He convulsed and buckled, falling backward into the building—permanently.

I quickly got back into my scope and scanned my sector. *Game on now.* All other thoughts departed my mind. Casanova scanned his sector, too.

Another Aidid militiaman carrying an AK-47 came out a fire escape door on the side of a building 300 yards away from me and aimed his rifle at the Delta operators assaulting the garage. From his position, I'm sure he thought he was safe from the assaulters, and he probably was. He was not safe from me—300 yards wasn't even a challenge. I shot him through his left side, and the round exited his right. He slumped down onto the fire escape landing, never knowing what hit him. His AK-47 lay silent next to him. Someone tried to reach out and retrieve the weapon. One round from my Win Mag put a stop to that.

Each time I made a shot, I immediately forgot about that target and scanned for another.

Chaos erupted inside and outside of the garage. People ran everywhere. Little Birds and Black Hawks filled the skies with deafening rotor blasts. I was in my own little world, though. Nothing existed outside my scope and my mission. Let the Unit guys handle their business in the garage. My business was reaching out and touching the enemy.

A few minutes passed as I continued scanning. More than 800 yards away, a guy popped up with an RPG launcher on his shoulder, preparing to fire at the helicopters.

If I took him out, it would be the longest killing shot of my career. If I failed . . .

2.
Hell Is for Children

My road to becoming a SEAL began in Boynton Beach, Florida. My mother had me there when she was sixteen years old—a child having a child—on November 8, 1961, in Weems Free Clinic. She couldn't afford a regular hospital. Born two months prematurely, I only weighed 3 pounds 2 ounces. The clinic was so poor that it didn't have the incubator a little one like me needed. I was so small that my mother literally carried me home in a shoe box. I slept in a dresser drawer padded with a blanket.

My mother, Millie Kirkman, was hardheaded and inflexible. She didn't show emotion. She worked hard every day in a sewing factory to help support my sisters and me. I probably inherited my hardheaded, refusing-to-quit-if-you-think-you're-right attitude from her—to a fault.

She told tell me that Ben Wilbanks, my biological father, had run off and abandoned us. I hated him for that.

The earliest memory I have of my childhood is in West Palm Beach, Florida, when I was four years old—awakened in the middle of the night by a huge man reeking of liquor. His name was Leon, and my mother was dating him. She first met Leon while working as a waitress at a truck stop.

They had just come back from a date. Leon snatched me out of the top bunk, questioning me about why I'd done something wrong that day. Then he slapped me around, hitting me in the face, to the point where I could taste my own blood. That was Leon's way of helping my mother keep her male child on the straight and narrow.

This was only the beginning. It didn't always happen at night. Whenever Leon came to the house, he took it upon himself to discipline me. I was terrified, dreading Mom's next date—literally shaking. My heart felt as though it would beat out of my chest. *How bad is it going to be this time?* A beating could happen when Leon arrived at the house while my mother got ready or when they came home. Leon wasn't picky about when he let me have it.

One day after kindergarten, I ran away. On purpose, I got on the wrong school bus. *This guy isn't going to beat me anymore. I'm outta here.* The bus took me out in the country somewhere. I had no idea where I was. There were only a few kids left on the bus. It stopped. A kid stood up. I followed him off the bus. The kid walked down the dirt road to his house. I didn't know what to do at that point—at five years old, I hadn't put a lot of thought into it. I walked down the dirt road until I got to the house at the end. Then I hung around outside not knowing what to do except stay away from the main road.

After a couple of hours, a man and a woman came home to find me sitting on the back porch, staying out of sight from the main road. The woman asked, "What's your name?"

"Howard."

"You must be hungry." They took me in and fed me.

Later, the woman said, "You know, we got to get hold of your parents. Get you back home."

"No, no," I said. "Please, please don't call my mom. Is there any way I could just live here with y'all?"

They laughed.

I didn't know what was so funny, but I didn't tell them the situation. "No, don't call my mom. Can I just live here with y'all?"

"No, honey. You don't understand. Your mama's probably worried sick. What's your phone number?"

I honestly didn't know.

"Where do you live?"

I tried to tell them how to get to my house, but the bus had taken so many turns that I couldn't remember. Finally, they took me back to my school. There they found my aunt looking for me.

My escape plan had failed. I lied to my mom, telling her I got on the wrong bus by accident.

Within a year or two, my mom married Leon. Soon afterward, we moved to Screven, Georgia, and we went to see the judge there. In the car, my mother said, "When we see the judge, he's going to ask you if you want Mr. Leon to be your daddy. You're supposed to tell him yes." Leon was the last thing in the world I wanted in my life, but I knew damn well I better say yes, because if I didn't, I'd probably be killed when we got home. So I did my duty.

The next day, before I went to school, my parents told me, "You tell them at school you're not a Wilbanks anymore—you're a Wasdin." So I did.

Now I was the adopted child and had to see Leon every day. When a lion acquires a lioness with cubs, he kills them. Leon didn't kill me, but anything that was not done exactly right, I paid for. Sometimes even when things were done right, I paid.

We had pecan trees in the yard. It was my job to pick up the pecans. Leon was a truck driver, and when he came home, if he heard any pecans pop under his wheels, he smacked me. Didn't matter if any had fallen since I had picked them all up. When I got home from school, I'd have to go straight to the bedroom and lie down on the bed, and Leon would mercilessly beat me with a belt.

The next day at school, whenever I used the toilet, I would have to peel my underwear away from the blood and scabs on my butt to sit down. I never got mad at God, but sometimes I asked Him for help: "God, please kill Leon."

After so much, it got to the point that when the 250-pound man's belt cut across my lower back, butt, and legs, I wasn't afraid anymore. *Calm down. Stop shaking. It isn't going to make it any better or any worse. Just take it.* I could literally lie there on the bed, close down, and block out the pain. That zombielike state only pissed off Leon more.

Dad and his older brother, my uncle Carroll, owned a watermelon field where I started working after school and during the summer. Those two were all about work. When they weren't working their farm, they were driving trucks. As I started contributing to the family, my relationship with Dad, who had stopped drinking, improved.

In South Georgia, where the heat exceeded 100 degrees and the humidity neared 100 percent, I would walk through the field cutting 30-pound watermelons off the vine, place them in a line to throw them over to the road, and then toss them up onto the pickup truck. One of the older guys would back the truck up to the trailer of an 18-wheeler, where I helped pack the watermelons onto the rig. After loading thousands of watermelons, I'd ride on the truck up to Columbia, South Carolina, in the early hours of the next morning to unload and sell the watermelons. I'd get about two hours of sleep before riding back.

When there was an hour or two to spare, my family would sometimes go for a picnic. On one of these picnics, I taught myself how to swim in the slow-moving waters of the Little Satilla River. I had no swimming technique whatsoever, but I felt at home in the water. We went there on a number of weekends: swimming and fishing for largemouth bass, crappie, redbreast, and bluegill.

Occasionally, after working in the watermelon patch, the crew and I went blackwater swimming in Lake Grace. Because of all the tannic acid from the pine trees and other vegetation, both the Little Satilla River and Lake Grace are so black on a good day that you can't see your feet in the water. In the summer, dragonflies hunt down mosquitoes. From the surrounding woods, squirrels chirp, ducks quack, and wild turkeys squawk. Those dark waters hold a mysterious beauty.

After work one day, the watermelon crew and I had a contest to see who could swim the farthest from the pier underwater at Lake Grace. As I swam beneath the surface of the dark brown water, I breathed out a little air. When I came up, someone said, "You had to be farting. There's no way you had that much air in your lungs."

Dad didn't mind if we spent a few hours swimming or fishing, but we never went hunting. My dad let me shoot his gun once in a while, but hunting was an all-day event. That would take too much time away from work. Work was his focus. If I made a mistake or didn't work hard enough, he beat me.

In junior high school, I hurt my leg playing football in gym class. One of the coaches said, "Let me check your hip out." He pulled my pants down so he could examine my right hip. He saw the hell that covered me from my lower back down to my upper legs where my dad had recently beaten me. The coach gasped. "Oh, my . . ." After checking my hip, he pulled my pants up and never said another word. In those days, whatever happened in the home stayed in the home. I remember feeling so embarrassed that someone had discovered my secret.

Despite everything, I loved my parents. It wasn't entirely their fault they were uneducated and didn't know how to nurture children. It was all they could do to put food on the table and keep four kids clothed. For the most part, my parents never used bad language. They were God-fearing people. Mom took my sisters and me to church every Sunday. They saw nothing wrong with their child-rearing skills.

Two men filled in with encouragement that probably saved my life. One was Brother Ron, pastor of First Baptist Church. I once got in a fight with another kid right in front of his church, starting a feud between our families that lasted weeks and nearly turned to shooting before Brother Ron got everyone to make peace. I believed in Brother Ron and looked up to him. He was like the town celebrity. Brother Ron was the glue that held the community together, and the community helped shape who I was.

Besides Brother Ron, another man who influenced me was Uncle Carroll. He didn't have Dad's hot temper. He may not have been well educated, but he was intelligent—especially in his dealings with people. Uncle Carroll had friends everywhere. He taught me how to drive a truck because Leon didn't have the patience. Leon would be angry at the first mistake I made picking watermelons, driving, or anything—it didn't matter. Uncle Carroll took the time to explain things. Being around Uncle Carroll, I learned people skills. Uncle Carroll was the only one who ever showed me any affection. On occasion, he'd put his arm around my shoulders if he knew Leon had been on my tail unrelentingly the way he usually was. He gave moral support, even a kind word on occasion. Through everything, Uncle Carroll's support was priceless. The best thing was that Uncle Carroll gave me words of encouragement. His influence was as critical as Brother Ron's, maybe even more. Without them, I would've harbored some dark thoughts. Probably suicide.

I spent my high school years as an Air Force Junior Reserve Officer Training Corps (JROTC) geek. I loved JROTC, with its discipline, structure, and nice uniform. I was always the outstanding cadet: ranking officer, color guard commander. It gave me something to do and excel at. The light came on, and I learned that I could lead pretty easily.

When it came to girls, though, I was a late bloomer. In October, I needed a date for the JROTC military ball. My JROTC buddy had a sister named Dianne; everyone called her Dee Dee. I hadn't really thought about her, but now I figured maybe she would go with me to the ball. Scared and embarrassed, I asked her, "Will you go to the military ball with me?"

"Yes," she said. We dated the rest of the school year until spring. Then the prom was coming, but someone had already asked Dee Dee to it. During home economics class, I asked her friend Laura to the prom—our first date. Because I grew up in a family that didn't show affection, her interest in me meant a lot.

When I graduated from high school, I stood 5'11" tall, and I'd saved up money for a car and Cumberland College in Williamsburg, Kentucky—a Christian school—but my sister Tammy totaled my car before I even left home, so I had to take the bus. At the station my mother told Dad, "Hug Howard." Then she told me, "Go hug your daddy." Leon put his arms out. We did an awkward hug. It was the first time we had ever hugged each other. Then I had a rare hug with my mother. I got on the bus glad to get the hell out of there.

After a year and a half of college, I had used up the last of my hard-earned money and couldn't afford to go back to school. I decided to visit the military recruiters at the shopping mall in Brunswick, Georgia. My plan was to join, save enough money, and return to college. A poster of a Search and Rescue (SAR) swimmer in a wetsuit hung outside the navy recruiter's office. That's as far as my dreaming went. I was twenty.

Before shipping out, I decided to marry Laura. Laura's family acted much different from my family. The kids and the parents *talked*. They had conversations. The parents were nice to the kids. Her father even told them good morning. That blew me away. They were loving and affectionate. I loved what their family had as much as I loved Laura. I had lacked a role model for being a husband and father. Dad never put his arm around my mother or held her hand. Maybe he did when I wasn't around, but I never saw it. Most of their conversation had only been about work or us kids. Doing things like telling Laura I loved her and holding her hand were difficult.

My parents grudgingly attended the small wedding. They didn't like Laura, but we lived in a town where it would've reflected poorly on them if they hadn't come. After Laura and I exchanged vows, my dad gave me a hundred-dollar bill and shook my hand without saying anything—no "Congratulations" or "Go to hell." Needless to say, my parents didn't stay for cake.

Boot camp was in Orlando, Florida. Two days after arriving, we all had fresh buzz cuts and smelled like denim. At lights-out, I told the guy in the bunk below me, "Hey, today was my birthday."

"Yeah, man. Happy birthday." He didn't give a crap. No one did. It was a bit of a reality check.

The lack of discipline and respect among the recruits amazed me. So many got in trouble for forgetting to say "Yes, sir" or "No, sir." I was raised to never forget my manners and never forget attention to detail. The guys doing extra duty—push-ups, stripping and waxing the floor—looked like fools. *Making your bed and folding your underwear isn't rocket science.* I was raised to make my bed and fold my underwear, and the punishment for forgetting was a lot worse than push-ups. I didn't know how much I'd already been prepared for the extremes a SEAL faces.

The company commander and I developed a bond—he'd had

the same Search and Rescue job as an air crewman that I wanted. He put me in charge of half the barracks. After finishing almost four weeks of boot camp, a quarter of the recruits were still having problems. I couldn't understand it.

Anyone who got in serious trouble had to go to Intensive Training (IT). I told my company commander, "I want to go to IT to get in shape for my Search and Rescue physical screening test, sir." I don't remember what the exact SAR requirements were then, but today's candidates must swim 500 yards in 13 minutes, run 1.5 miles in 12.5 minutes, do 35 push-ups in 2 minutes, perform 50 sit-ups in 2 minutes, and do 2 pull-ups. If I failed the test, I would miss my big reason for joining the navy—Search and Rescue.

My company commander looked at me like I had a mushroom growing out of my head. "Wasdin, do you know what they do at IT?"

"The guys that got in trouble told me they do a lot of exercise."

He laughed.

After evening chow, I arrived at IT and found out why he was laughing. IT busted my rump. We did push-ups, sit-ups, drills holding rifles over our heads, and much more. I looked to the left and to the right—the men on either side of me were crying. *This is tough, but why are you crying?* The people who ran IT didn't know I had volunteered for it. I never told them any different. When I left boot camp, they must've thought, *Wasdin was the biggest screwup who ever came through here.*

I took the Search and Rescue screening test. At the pool, I saw a guy with an unfamiliar insignia on his chest: An eagle and an anchor, with the eagle holding an antique pistol in one claw and a trident in another. I was too focused on the test to ask about it, but I didn't forget it.

The IT may have helped me—if not physically, mentally. I passed. Toward the end of the three-month navy boot camp, my air crewman company commander gave me a smile and orders to attend aircrew school. "I'll see you in the fleet," he said. I'd passed. That was the best day of my life.

Laura lived in our town while I attended aircrew school in Pensacola, Florida. At aircrew school, I got to wear flight suits, learned how to deploy the rescue raft out of an aircraft, ran the obstacle course, and boxed in informal navy tournaments. Toward the end of the six-week-long school, I attended a week of survival training. The instructors simulated our aircraft being shot down, and we had to survive: tie knots, cross a river, and build a tent out of a parachute, with only minimal food like broth and apples. During the last three days of the survival training, we only ate what we could find and were willing to put in our mouths. I wasn't ready to eat grub worms yet.

After aircrew school, some fellow trainees and I moved down the street and started twelve weeks of Search and Rescue school. The place was intimidating: names on the wall, gigantic indoor pool, mock door of an H-3 helicopter, and SAR instructors in their shorts and blue T-shirts.

Man, these guys are gods.

We got comfortable being in the water, jumped in with all our gear on, swam to the rescue hoist, hooked our pilot to it, did hand signals, lit the Mark-13 flare, and simulated rescues. SAR graduation was more special than boot camp or aircrew graduation because SAR training seriously challenged me physically and mentally.

After antisubmarine warfare and more practice on all these new skills, I reported to my first real duty station at HS-7 Squadron— the "Dusty Dogs." We were assigned to the aircraft carrier USS *John F. Kennedy* (CV-67).

Along with this, my son, Blake, was born. I was so proud to be a father and an elite SAR swimmer. Life was good.

3.
Russian Sub and Green Hero

On October 6, 1986, a Russian Yankee-class nuclear submarine (K-219) sailing off the coast of Bermuda experienced a failed seal on the missile hatch. Seawater leaked in and reacted with the missile liquid fuel residue, causing an explosion that killed three of its sailors. The sub limped toward Cuba. The *John F. Kennedy*'s task force sent my helicopter out to track the Russian vessel. Usually, we were supposed to fly within approximately 30 miles of our carrier group, but we had special permission to fly out farther.

I wore my booties, a short-sleeve wetsuit top called a shorty, and my white cotton briefs—tighty-whiteys. Most guys wore wetsuit bottoms, but I took my chances that I might have to rescue someone in my tighty-whiteys. For outerwear, I wore my flight suit. We picked up the Russian sub on active sonar. Following close, we kept popping its butt with sonar pings.

Suddenly, our pilot said, "Look at the temperature gauge on our main rotor transmission."

Oh, my . . . The gears burned hot enough to shear off.

The pilot tried to take us to a hover just before we fell out of the sky. We didn't hit the water as hard as I expected, but we hit hard enough. "Mayday, mayday . . ."

As the first swimmer, I rushed to the copilot to help him launch the sea anchor—a kind of parachute that floats underwater and acts as a brake, like the parachutes behind drag racers. Next, I made sure the pilot and copilot exited the aircraft through the front escape window. Then I hurried to the rear of the cockpit, where I made sure the first crewman had exited the side door. I took off my flight suit and put my swim fins, mask, and snorkel on. Finally, I kicked the raft out, inflated it, and helped the two pilots in. The other rescue swimmer was an older guy, in his forties. Instead of inflating his life vest and swimming to the raft, he hung on to a cooler for dear life, drifting out to sea. So I had to swim him down, bring him back to the raft, and get him inside. A disturbing thought occurred to me: *What am I going to do if that Russian sub rises up underneath us?*

An antisubmarine jet, an S-3 Viking, flew over, noting our position. Thirty minutes later, a helicopter arrived. I took the green sea dye marker, which looked like a bar of soap, and swished it in the water around the raft. We became a huge fluorescent green target for the rescue helicopter to see.

The helicopter came in low, and I signaled for them not to jump their swimmer. I put the pilots' helmet visors down to protect them from the stinging sea spray the helicopter blades blasted. Then I swam everyone over to the rescue hoist, riding up myself with the last guy.

Our rescue helicopter landed on the aircraft carrier. We stepped out onto the flight deck, and everyone cheered, slapping me on the back, congratulating me for the rescue. Walking across the flight deck, I carried my swim fins, looking like the hero, except for my tighty-whiteys. Now my cotton briefs were tighty-fluorescent-greeneys. My whole body glowed from the fluorescent green dye marker. It was embarrassing as hell. I would've given a million dollars for my wetsuit bottom. Later, to my horror, others and I watched the scene all over again on the ship's video.

* * *

A couple of weeks before my active duty contract with the navy expired, I noticed five guys from a unit I'd never heard of: SEALs. They were in our Search and Rescue berthing space, so I started following them around asking questions about the SEALs.

During World War II, the first navy frogmen were trained to recon beaches for amphibious landings. Soon they learned underwater demolitions to clear obstacles and became known as Underwater Demolition Teams (UDTs). In the Korean War, UDTs evolved and went farther inland, blowing up bridges and tunnels.

Years later, after observing Communist insurgency in Southeast Asia, President John F. Kennedy—who had served in the navy during World War II—and others in the military understood the need for unconventional warriors. On January 1, 1962, SEAL Team One (Coronado, California) and SEAL Team Two (Little Creek, Virginia) were born.

One of the first SEALs was Rudy Boesch, a New Yorker and chief from UDT-21. Wearing his hair in a perfect crew cut, he led the newly formed SEALs at Team Two in physical training (PT). On his dog tag in the space for RELIGION was written PT. To stay in shape, Rudy and his Teammates played soccer for hours—thirty-two men on each team. Broken legs were common. The SEALs used a variety of tactics to get out of Rudy's fitness runs—making excuses, going to the restroom and not returning, and ducking into the bushes during the runs.

Rudy also served as chief of 10th Platoon in the Vietnam War. The SEALs' meat and potatoes were snatch-and-grabs. At night, Rudy and his Teammates crept into a thatched hut and grabbed one of the Vietcong (VC) out of his hammock. The SEALs turned him over to the CIA or the South Vietnamese police for interrogation. Then Rudy and his Teammates would act on that intelligence the next evening and snatch a VC who was higher up in the food chain.

By the end of the war, SEAL Teams One and Two had been decorated with 3 Medals of Honor, 2 Navy Crosses, 42 Silver Stars, 402 Bronze Stars (one of them Rudy's), and numerous other awards. For every SEAL killed, they killed two hundred. In the late seventies, Rudy helped in the formation of Mobility Six (MOB Six), SEAL Team Two's counterterrorist unit.

The SEALs on the *John F. Kennedy* probably got tired of me, but they shared some of the horror stories of Basic Underwater Demolition/SEAL (BUD/S) Training. They told me about sky-diving, scuba diving, shooting, and blowing things up—and catching shrimp in the Delta. They worked hard and played hard. Lots of camaraderie. I thought I'd joined an elite unit before, but now I knew about a unit that was more elite. There would be no satisfaction staying where I was. I wanted what they had.

One told me that he got his orders to BUD/S as an incentive to reenlist in the navy when his contract was done. Talk about divine intervention—meeting the right people at the right time. I asked my commanding officer for the same thing.

"Get your ass in here." He opened the door to his office. "You don't know what you're asking. BUD/S is not what you really want to do. Take your money, go back home, and finish your education. You have no idea what it takes to become a SEAL." He spent the better part of an hour telling me what a crazy thing I was asking.

I thanked him politely and a few days later started to get ready to head home to become a civilian again. A day before catching my flight home I was already on shore and just planning some final sightseeing when I learned he'd put in for me to go to BUD/S and my orders had arrived.

The orders were contingent on me passing the physical screening test for BUD/S in Jacksonville. I flew back home to Georgia, and Laura drove me down to Florida. During the nearly six months

I'd spent on a deployed aircraft carrier, I didn't have much time to swim—except for rescuing the crew of my crashed helicopter. Before that, I mostly swam with fins on. The test was without fins. I hadn't practiced the sidestroke and breaststroke required for SEAL training, either. Although I don't remember the exact physical screening test requirements when the SEALs tested me, they were similar to today's: a 500-yard swim within 12.5 minutes, rest 10 minutes, 42 push-ups in 2 minutes, rest 2 minutes, 50 sit-ups in 2 minutes, rest 2 minutes, 6 pull-ups before dropping off the bar, rest 10 minutes, run 1.5 miles wearing boots and trousers within 11.5 minutes.

Twelve of us showed our IDs and paperwork. Then we stripped down to our swim shorts. I was nervous. At the sound of the whistle, we swam. As I neared the end of the 500-yard swim, the SEAL called out the time remaining, "Thirty seconds." Fighting to swim against each second, I finally reached the end with only fifteen seconds to spare. One applicant was not as fortunate.

Eleven of us got dressed in T-shirts, long pants, and boots. We did our push-ups and sit-ups. Again, I passed. Two more applicants failed.

After the two-minute rest, I jumped up on the pull-up bar. The stress of failure can sometimes cause people to implode. I passed, and two others failed.

Only seven of us remained. Each activity by itself wasn't so difficult, but doing one after the other *was*. We stepped onto the running track. The SEAL wished us good luck. I passed. One guy failed. Out of the twelve of us who started, only six of us were left.

The cuts didn't stop there. Some applicants didn't score high enough on the Armed Services Vocational Aptitude Battery (AS-VAB), the intelligence test all potential recruits take before entering the military. During dental, medical, and hyperbaric chamber tests, more guys failed. Some guys failed for poor vision or being color-blind. Others failed the psychology testing. One psychology questionnaire asked the same questions over and over. I wasn't sure if they were checking the reliability of the test or my patience, but I passed.

For the hyperbaric pressure testing, the chamber was a large torpedo-looking thing that simulated going down 60 feet under-water and staying there. Some guys freaked out during the testing—the claustrophobia, air pressure, or both got to them. I stepped inside, sat down, and relaxed: slow breathing, slow heartbeat. No problem.

Out of a hundred applicants, I was the only one who passed all the tests. I was beyond excited.

4.
The Only Easy Day
Was Yesterday

When I showed up at the Naval Special Warfare Center in Coronado, California, I walked over the sand berm and saw the Pacific Ocean for the first time. Huge waves crashed in. *Holy crap.* I jumped into the balmy California water. It wasn't balmy—especially in comparison to the Florida gulf waters I'd trained in. *That's freezing.* I popped out quicker than I'd jumped in. *Wonder how much time we're going to have to spend in that.*

On the first morning of indoctrination into BUD/S, we had to do the physical screening test again. After a cold shower and some push-ups, we began the test. One guy failed; he hung his head as the instructors sent him packing.

That evening, the SEAL instructors stood before us and introduced themselves. At the end, Lieutenant Moore told us we could quit if we wanted to by walking outside and ringing the bell three times.

"I'll wait," Lieutenant Moore said.

I thought the lieutenant was bluffing, but some of my classmates began ringing the bell.

A number of my remaining classmates were impressive: an Iron Man triathlete, a college football player, and others. One evening in the barracks, I looked at myself in the mirror. *These guys are like racehorses. What the hell am I doing here?*

23

The next day, Iron Man rang the bell. I couldn't understand why.

One of our first training evolutions included the obstacle course (O-course). One night a SEAL might have to exit a submerged submarine, hang on for dear life as his Zodiac inflatable boat jumps over waves, scale a cliff, hump through enemy territory to his objective, scale a three-story building, do his deed, and get the hell out. The O-course helps prepare a man for that kind of work. It has also broken more than one trainee's neck or back—climbing over the top of the 60-foot cargo net is a bad time to lose arm strength. Much of our training was dangerous, and injuries were common.

We lined up in alphabetical order by our last names. I stood near the end, watching everyone take off before me. When my turn came, I took off like a cruise missile. I couldn't understand why I was passing so many people.

Partway through, I ran to the bottom of a three-story tower. I jumped up and grabbed the ledge to the second floor, then swung my legs up. I jumped up and grabbed the ledge to the third floor, then swung my legs up. Then I came back down. As I moved on to more obstacles, I noticed someone stuck behind on the three-story tower. There stood Mike W., who had played football at the University of Alabama, tears of frustration streaming down his face because he couldn't make it to the third floor.

With a hint of Georgia in his accent, Instructor Stoneclam yelled, "You can run up and down a college football field, but you can't get up to the top of one obstacle. You sissy!"

I wondered what the hell was wrong with Mike W. He was in way better shape than I was. *Wasn't he?* (Mike would severely injure his back, but Captain Bailey kept him around doing therapy for almost a year. Later, he became an outstanding SEAL officer.)

A number of the racehorses were the biggest crybabies. They'd probably been number one much of their lives, and now when they had their first taste of adversity—BUD/S style—they couldn't handle it.

What the hell is wrong with these prima donnas?

Although running and swimming came hard for me, the obstacle course turned out to be one of my favorite events. Bobby H. and I were always pushing each other out of the number one ranking. Instructor Stoneclam advised a student, "Look how Wasdin attacks the obstacles."

I'd rather be doing this than picking watermelons.

The sun lay buried in the horizon as we marched double-time through the Naval Amphibious Base across the street. Wearing the same green uniforms, we sang out in cadence, looking confident, but the tension in the air was thick. *If anybody is going to die, this is going to be the time.*

We arrived at the pool located at Building 164 and stripped down to our UDT swim shorts. An instructor said, "You are going to love this. Drown-proofing is one of my favorites. Sink or swim, sweet peas."

I tied my feet together, and my swim partner tied my hands behind my back.

"When I give the command, the bound men will hop into the deep end of the pool," Instructor Stoneclam said. "You must bob up and down twenty times, float for five minutes, swim to the shallow end of the pool, turn around without touching the bottom, swim back to the deep end, do a forward and backward somersault underwater, and retrieve a face mask from the bottom of the pool with your teeth."

The hardest part for me was swimming the length of the pool

and back with my feet tied together and hands tied behind my back. I had to flip around like a dolphin. *Even so, I'd rather be doing this than being awakened from a dead sleep and slapped around.*

We lost a muscular guy who just sank like a rock to the bottom of the pool. A skinny redheaded hospital corpsman jumped in the water, but instead of swimming straight, he swam in a horseshoe. An instructor told him, "Swim in a straight line. What the hell is wrong with you?" The instructors found out later that Redhead was almost blind. He had forged his medical records to get to BUD/S.

For every guy who would do anything to get in, there were guys who wanted to get out. Stoneclam wouldn't let them.

"You can't quit now!" Instructor Stoneclam screamed. "This is only Indoc [Indoctrination]. Training hasn't even started yet!"

After three weeks of Indoc, we began First Phase, Basic Conditioning. Our class continued to shrink due to performance failures, injuries, and quitting. Woe to the trainee who let the pain show in his face. An instructor would say, "You didn't like that? Well, do some more." Likewise to the trainee who showed no pain. "You liked that? Here's another kick in the crotch." We ran a mile one-way just to eat a meal. Round-trip multiplied by three meals made for 6 miles a day just to eat! We never seemed to have enough time to recover before the next evolution hit us. On top of everything, the instructors poured on the stress with verbal harassment.

Each one of us seemed to have an Achilles' heel—and the instructors excelled at finding it. The hardest evolutions for me were the 4-mile timed runs on the beach wearing long pants and jungle boots. I dreaded them. With each run, the time demands became tougher. Almost every time, at the 2-mile marker at the North Island fence, an instructor would say, "Wasdin, you're getting behind."

I failed one 4-mile timed run by seconds. While everyone else went back to the barracks, the four or five others who also failed joined me to form a goon squad—our name for the guys who were punished or made to do extra duty because they didn't pass the first time. We ran sprints up and down the sand berm, jumped into the cold water, then did all manner of acrobatic tortures until the sand rubbed our wet skin raw and nearly every muscle in our bodies broke down. It was my first goon squad—and the only one I ever needed. *I may die on the next timed run, but I ain't doin' this crap again.* There was one guy who swam like a fish but ended up in goon squad time and time again for not keeping up on the runs. I wondered how he ever survived all the goon squads.

In First Phase, one thing sucked more than the four-mile timed runs: Hell Week—the ultimate in *train the best, discard the rest.*

It began late Sunday night with what is called breakout. M-60 machine guns blasted the air. We crawled out of the barracks as an instructor screamed, "Move, move, move!"

Outside, artillery simulators exploded—an incoming shriek followed by a boom. M-60s continued to rattle. A machine pumped a blanket of fog over the area. Green chemlights, glow sticks, decorated the outer perimeter. Water hoses sprayed us. The smell of cordite hung in the air. Over the loudspeakers blasted AC/DC's "Highway to Hell."

Terror covered the faces of many guys. Only minutes into it, the bell started ringing—people quit. *You can't be serious. What the hell's wrong?* Of course, my tough childhood had prepared me for this moment. More than physically, I knew that mentally I had mastered pain and hard work, and I knew I could master more. In my mind, I strongly believed I wouldn't quit.

One legendary Hell Week event occurs on a steel pier where the navy docks its small boats. Wearing our olive drab green uniforms, we jumped into the bay with no life jackets, shoes, or socks. I immediately laid out facedown in a dead man's float while I pulled off my trousers. I tied the legs together with a square knot. Then, using both hands, I grabbed hold of the waist and kicked until my body straightened up from its float. I lifted my pants high in the air, then slammed them forward and down on the water, trapping air in the trouser legs to make a flotation device. I rested my chest in the V of my floating pants, felt relief for a moment, then started to remember the cold.

Some of our guys swam back to the pier. We tried to call them back, but they'd had enough. *Ring, ring, ring.*

Instructor Stoneclam said, "If one more of you rings the bell, the rest of you can come out of the water, too. Inside the ambulance we have warm blankets and a thermos of hot coffee."

After one more ring of the bell, Stoneclam said, "Everybody out of the water!"

"Hooyah!"

We crawled out of the water and onto the floating steel pier.

Instructor Stoneclam said, "Now strip down to your undershorts and lie down on the pier. If you don't have shorts, your birthday suit is even better."

I stripped down to my birthday suit and lay down. The instructors had prepared the pier by spraying it down with water. Mother Nature had prepared the pier by blowing cool wind across it. I felt like I was lying down on a block of ice. Then the instructors sprayed us with cold water. Our muscles contracted wildly. The spasms were uncontrollable. We flapped around on the steel deck like fish out of water.

The instructors took us to the early stages of hypothermia. I would've done almost anything to get warm. Mike said, "Sorry, man, I gotta pee."

"It's OK, man. Pee here."

He urinated on my hands.

"Oh, thanks, buddy." The warmth felt so good.

Most people think it's just gross—they've obviously never been *really* cold.

Wednesday night—halfway through Hell Week—was the one time I thought about quitting. Lyon's Lope, named after a Vietnam SEAL, is a test that combines several stages of paddling a boat—sometimes by hand—with stages of long runs. When we finished, we all had Stage Two hypothermia. Stage One is mild to strong shivering with numbness in the hands—most people have experienced this level of hypothermia. Stage Two is violent shivering with mild confusion and stumbling. In Stage Three, the core body temperature drops below 90 degrees, shivering stops, and a person becomes a babbling, bumbling idiot. There is no Stage Four—only death. The instructors calculated air and water temperatures along with how long we stayed in the water, to make us as cold as possible without causing permanent damage or killing us.

It was standing room only at the bell. My classmates rang it like Coronado was on fire. The instructors had backed up ambulances and opened the doors. Inside sat my former classmates wrapped up in wool blankets drinking hot chocolate. Instructor Stoneclam said, "Come here, Wasdin. You're married, aren't you?"

"Yes, Instructor Stoneclam." My muscles felt too exhausted to move, but they shivered violently anyway.

"You don't need this. Come here." He walked me to the backs of the ambulances, so I could feel their warm air hit me in the face. "Have a cup of this hot chocolate."

I held it in my hand. It was warm.

"If we'd wanted you to have a wife, we would've issued you one," he explained. "Go over there and ring that damn bell. Get this over. I'll let you drink that hot chocolate. Put you in this warm ambulance. Wrap you up in a thick blanket. And you don't have to put up with this anymore."

I looked over at the bell. *It would be that easy. All I have to do is pull that mother three times.* I thought about the heated ambulances with blankets and hot chocolate. Then I caught myself. *Wait a minute. I'm not thinking clearly. That's quitting.* "Hooyah, Instructor Stoneclam." I gave him back his hot chocolate.

"Get back with your class."

Handing him back that cup of hot chocolate was the hardest thing I'd ever done. *Let me go back and freeze while I get my nuts kicked some more.*

Mike H. and I had a six-man boat crew before the other four quit. Now it was only the two of us struggling to drag our boat, weighing nearly 200 pounds, back to the BUD/S compound—instructors yelling at us for being too slow. We cussed at the quitters. "You sorry pieces of crap." When Mike and I arrived at the compound, we were still angry.

Mike and I had gone from being their comrades to cussing them out for abandoning us. It's why the training is so brutal. To find out who has your back when all hell breaks loose. After Wednesday night, I don't remember anyone else quitting.

Early Thursday morning, I sat in the chow hall. *They're going to have to kill me. After everything I've been through, they're going to have to cut me up in little pieces and mail me back to Wayne County, Georgia, because I'm not quitting now.* Inside me, something clicked. It no longer mattered what we did next. I didn't care. *This has got to end sometime.*

Deprived of support in our environment and the support of our own bodies, the only thing propping us up was our belief in accomplishing the mission—complete Hell Week. In psychology this belief is called self-efficacy. Even when the mission seems impossible, it is the strength of our belief that makes success possible. The absence of this belief guarantees failure. Believing allows us to see the goal (complete Hell Week) and break the goal down into more manageable objectives (one evolution at a time). If the evolution is a boat race, it can be broken down into even smaller objectives such as paddling. Thinking too much about what happened and what is about to happen will wear you down. Live in the moment and take it one step at a time.

Thursday night, we'd only had three to four hours total sleep since Sunday evening. The dream world started to mix with the real world, and we hallucinated. In the chow hall, while guys' heads were bobbing in and out of their food and their eyes were rolling back in their heads from sleep deprivation, an instructor said, "You know, Wasdin, I want you to take this butter knife, go over there, and kill that deer in the corner."

Slowly rising from my oatmeal daze, I looked over and, sure as hell, there was a buck standing in the chow hall. It didn't dawn on me why the deer was in the chow hall or how it got there. *Now I'm on a mission.* I stalked up on it with my Rambo knife and got ready to make my death leap.

Instructor Stoneclam yelled, "Wasdin, what are you doing?"

"Getting ready to kill this buck, Instructor Stoneclam."

"Look, that's a tray table. It's what they haul trays in and out of the kitchen with."

What the . . . ? How did it turn into a tray table?

"Just sit your dumb ass down and finish eating," Instructor Stoneclam said.

The instructors had a big laugh about it.

One guy in our class, Randy Clendening wheezed and sputtered through Hell Week. He had fluid in his lungs. The instructors discussed rolling him back to another class so he could recover, but that would mean doing Hell Week again—and we were so close to finishing.

On Friday, the instructors took us out into the surf zone. We sat in the frigid ocean facing the sea with our arms linked, trying to stay together. Instructor Stoneclam stood on the beach talking to our backs. "This is the sorriest class we've ever seen. You couldn't even keep the officers in your class. You didn't support them. You didn't back them up. This last evolution, you had the slowest time in history. We have just received permission to extend Hell Week one more day."

He was messing with us. When he ordered us to turn around to face shore, we saw our commanding officer, Captain Larry Bailey. "Congratulations, men." Hell Week was over.

Some of the others jumped for joy—I was hurting too bad for that kind of celebration. Randy Clendening cried tears of relief; he'd made it through with walking pneumonia. I stood there with a dumb look on my face. *What am I doing here?* I looked around. *Where did everybody go?* We'd started with ten or twelve boat crews, six to eight men in each. Now we only had four or five boat crews. *Why did those guys even start Hell Week if they knew they didn't want it?* They didn't know they didn't want it.

Medical personnel took Randy directly to the infirmary to ventilate him. They screened the rest of us. We were examined for "flesh-eating bacteria." (Actually, the bacteria release toxins that destroy skin and muscle rather than eating them.) With cuts and bruises covering our bodies from head to toe, we were meals on wheels for the killer bacteria. Some of the guys had different kinds of infections that had traveled from cuts to deep inside the skin. Others had strained their leg and hip muscles so badly that they could barely walk.

I took a shower, then drank some Gatorade. In the barracks,

I lay down and went to sleep. People kept watch on us while we slept to make sure we didn't swallow our tongues, drown in our spit, or simply stop breathing due to fatigue.

The next day, I rolled over on the top rack of my bunk bed and jumped off the way I always did, but my legs weren't working. My face hit the deck, giving me a bloody nose and lip.

As we hobbled into the chow hall, all eyes seemed to be on us. We were the ones who had just made it through "the week." It had been the coldest week in twenty-three years. It had actually hailed in Southern California.

The guys who had quit during Hell Week avoided eye contact. I had begged one of them not to ring out, but he abandoned Mike and me to carry that boat by ourselves. *Could've at least waited to quit until after we got that boat back to the barracks.* He walked over to my table. "I'm sorry, man. I know I let you guys down, but I just couldn't do it anymore."

I looked up at him. "Get out of my face."

Training resumed slowly, starting with a lot of stretching exercises. Then it picked up speed. Time limits tightened. Distances increased. More swims, runs, and obstacle course trials. Academic tests continued. Pre–Hell Week, we had focused on topics such as first aid and boat handling. Now we focused on hydrographic reconnaissance. Enlisted men like me had to score 70 percent or higher. Officer standards were 80 percent or higher, although we had already lost all our officers.

A new evolution we had to pass was the 50-meter underwater swim. At the pool, Instructor Stoneclam said, "All of you have to swim fifty meters underwater. You'll do a somersault into the pool, so no one gets a diving start, and swim twenty-five meters across. Touch the end and swim twenty-five meters back. If you break the surface at any time, you fail. Don't forget to swim along the bottom. The increased pressure on your lungs will help you hold your breath longer, so you can swim farther."

As I neared the end, I began to black out. After I touched the wall, Instructor Stoneclam had to grab me by the waistband of my swim shorts and pull me out of the pool. Two guys failed their second chance and were expelled from training. (NOTE: Do not practice underwater swimming or breath holding at home because it *will* kill you.)

In Second Phase, Land Warfare, we learned covert infiltrations, sentry removal, handling agents/guides, gathering intelligence, snatching the enemy, performing searches, handling prisoners, shooting, blowing stuff up, etc. As a child, I learned attention to detail—making sure that not one single pecan remained on the ground when my dad came home saved my butt from getting whipped. Now, that same attention to detail would save my butt from getting shot or blown up. Attention to detail is why I would never have a parachute malfunction. I never so much as sprained a toe in 752 jumps.

In Third Phase, Dive Phase, we learned underwater navigation and techniques for sabotaging ships. Some of my classmates had trouble with dive physics and pool competency (pool comps). I had difficulty treading water with tanks on and keeping my fingers above the water for five minutes. An instructor would yell, "Get that other finger up, Wasdin!" So I would.

Toward the end of training, during one of our long runs, we ran behind a truck while music played. I actually visualized myself wearing the SEAL trident. *I'm either going home in a coffin or I'm going home wearing the trident. I'm going to make it through training.* It felt like a vision had opened up in my mind. It was the first and only time I got a runner's high. Some guys got that runner's high repeatedly. For me, it sucked every time I ran.

* * *

We ran before each meal on even days. On odd days, we did pull-ups before each meal. Randy Clendening always made the timed sprints but failed the pull-ups. Every other day he endured the punishment. He sat in the ocean with water up to his chest and ate his cold MRE for breakfast, lunch, and dinner. He wanted the program way more than I did.

After that, I risked trouble with the instructors to sneak food into the barracks for him on odd days. Other guys snuck him food, too. I have the greatest respect for guys like Randy who work harder than everyone else and somehow manage to finish BUD/S. More than the gazelles running ahead, more than the fish swimming in front, more than the monkeys swinging through the O-course—these underdogs were hardcore.

One of the most famous underdogs in SEAL history was Thomas Norris. He had wanted to join the FBI but got drafted instead. He joined the navy to become a pilot, but his eyesight disqualified him. So he volunteered for SEAL training, where he often fell to the rear on runs and swims. The instructors talked about dropping him from the program. Norris didn't give up and became a SEAL at Team Two. He won the Medal of Honor for rescuing a pilot after three other rescue missions had failed. He was unstoppable.

About six months after that rescue, he and four other men were stuck in North Vietnam, surrounded by North Vietnamese troops. They fought for five hours until they could contact a ship for help. At one point, Norris was shot in the face. The bullet entered the side of Norris's head and blew out the front of his forehead. He was dead. Petty Officer Michael Thornton of SEAL Team One threw the body on his shoulders in a fireman's carry to bring him home. Thornton himself was almost out of ammo. It looked like the end for him, too.

Suddenly, the first round of U.S. artillery came in from the

Newport News like a car flying through the air. When it exploded, it threw Thornton down a 30-foot dune. Norris's body flew over Thornton. He picked himself up and walked over to pick up Norris.

"Mike, buddy," Norris said.

"You sonofabitch. You're alive!"

Thornton lifted Norris up again, and carried him to the water's edge. At this point Thornton didn't notice that he'd been shot through his left calf himself. Thornton tried to bandage Norris's wound, but it was too large. Norris was going into shock. Thornton swam out for pickup with Norris in tow. It was a long time before he got Norris to a medical team on the *Newport News*. The doctors told him Norris wouldn't make it. He did. He held on long enough for them to evacuate him to the Philippines and then to a naval hospital back home. He underwent several major surgeries, as he had lost part of his skull and one eye. When the Navy retired him, he returned to his childhood dream: becoming an FBI agent. FBI Director William Webster said, "If you can pass the same test as anybody else applying for this organization, I will waiver your disabilities." Of course, Norris passed. He served in the FBI for twenty years. He never gave up.

Thornton received the Medal of Honor for his actions. Years later, he would help form SEAL Team Six and serve as one of its operators.

Some legends are passed down to BUD/S trainees, but I wouldn't learn about Norris until after I became a SEAL. In such a small, tight-knit community, a SEAL's reputation, good or bad, travels fast. That reputation begins at BUD/S. Norris remained the underdog throughout his careers in the Teams and the FBI. Now I had to forge my own reputation.

BUD/S prepares us to believe we can accomplish the mission—and to never surrender. No SEAL has ever been held prisoner of war. The only explicit training we receive in BUD/S is to look out for each other—leave no one behind. A lot of our tactical training deals with retreats, escape, and evasion. We are taught to be mentally tough, training repeatedly until our muscles can react automatically. Looking back, I now realize that my mental toughness training started at an early age. Our planning is meticulous, which shows in our briefings. In my encounters with the army, navy, air force, and marines, I've only seen Delta Force brief as well as we do.

A SEAL's belief in accomplishing the mission transcends environmental or physical obstacles that threaten to make him fail. Often we think we're indestructible. Forever the optimists, even when we're outnumbered and outgunned, we still tend to think we have a chance to make it out alive—and be home in time for dinner.

Nevertheless, sometimes a SEAL can't find his way back to Mother Ocean and must make a choice between fighting to the death or surrendering. For many brave warriors, it's better to roll the dice on surrendering in order to live to fight another day— SEALs have incredible respect for those POWs. As SEALs, though, we believe our surrender would be giving in, and giving in is never an option. I wouldn't want to be used as some political bargaining chip against the United States. I wouldn't want to die in a cage of starvation or have my head cut off for some video to be shown around the world on the Internet. My attitude is that if the enemy wants to kill me, they're going to have to kill me now. We despise would-be dictators who wish to dominate us—SEALs steer the rudders of their own destinies. Our world is a meritocracy where we are free to leave at any time. Our missions are voluntary; I can't think of a mission that wasn't. Ours is an unwritten code: It's better to burn out than to fade away—and with our last breaths we'll take as many of the enemy with us as possible.

* * *

Laura and Blake, who was just a toddler, flew out for my graduation. Blake rang the bell for me. I told him, "Now you never have to go to BUD/S, because you've already rung out." In his teenage years, he would want to become a SEAL, but I would talk him out of it. Half a dozen people in my hometown would have kids who wanted to go to BUD/S. I would talk every single one of them out of it. If I'm able to talk someone out of it, I'm just saving them time, because they really don't want it anyway. If I can't talk them out of it, maybe they really want it.

After BUD/S, we went directly to airborne training at Fort Benning, Georgia, home of the army's airborne and infantry schools. The summer was so hot that they had to run us through the sprinklers two or three times a day to cool us off. Even so, people still fell out from heatstroke and heat exhaustion. Some of the soldiers talked as if the training were the hardest thing in the world. They thought they were becoming part of some elite fighting force. Coming from BUD/S, airborne training was a joke.

Army regulations didn't allow the instructors to drop anyone for more than ten push-ups. One airborne instructor was a "good old boy" who always had a wad of Red Man chewing tobacco in his mouth. We tadpoles screwed around with him wanting more push-ups.

"Give me ten, Navy," he said.

We did ten push-ups, then stood up.

"Hell no." He spit his tobacco. "Too damn easy."

We dropped down and did ten more.

"Hell no. Too damn easy."

We did ten more.

At night, we went out drinking until late. For us, airborne training was a holiday. Now the real fun would begin.

5.
SEAL Team Two

After airborne training, I reported to my SEAL Team. The odd-numbered Teams (One, Three, and Five) were on the West Coast at Coronado, California, and the even-numbered Teams (Two, Four, and Eight) were on the East Coast at Little Creek, Virginia. Although the Top Secret SEAL Team Six existed, I knew nothing about it. I reported to SEAL Team Two in Little Creek.

This is where I met Rudy Boesch, who was still a SEAL despite being nearly sixty years old. During a Wednesday run on the obstacle course, I thought I could take it easy. There were no instructors around yelling at us. At the end of the course, Rudy pulled aside all of us who finished behind him. "Meet me back up here this afternoon."

That afternoon, the slowpokes and I ran the O-course again. It was a wake-up call. Even in the Teams, it paid to be a winner. Later, I would become one of the fastest men on the O-course at Team Two.

Rudy soon served as the first senior enlisted adviser of the newly formed United States Special Operations Command (USSOCOM), commanding navy, army, air force, and marine special operations units, including those in JSOC such as SEAL Team Six and Delta. After more than forty-five years in the navy, most of it as a SEAL, Rudy retired. When he reached his seventies, he competed on the reality TV series *Survivor*.

A few months after arriving, the fun began: advanced training in sea, air, and land warfare, known as SEAL Tactical Training (STT). While BUD/S focused on screening out people *and* training the survivors, STT mostly focused on training. During the six months of STT, only two people were dropped because of poor performance. We learned advanced levels of diving and land warfare, including close-quarters combat (CQC). (For more on advanced training after BUD/S, see Dick Couch's *The Finishing School*.)

When I completed STT, the SEAL Team Two skipper, Norm Carley, came out with tridents and pinned one on me. The trident consisted of an eagle clutching a U.S. Navy anchor, trident, and pistol. Because it looked like the old Budweiser eagle, we often called the trident "the Budweiser." Both officers and enlisted wore the same gold badge, rather than following the common navy practice of making enlisted men wear silver. It is still one of the biggest, gaudiest badges in the navy. With his fist, Skipper gave it a smack on my chest. Then each member of my platoon came by and punched it in. The trident literally stuck so deep into my chest that the leading petty officer had to pull it out of my skin. The marks remained on me for weeks. Now I could officially play with the big boys.

I took my first deployment with SEAL Team Two to Machrihanish, Scotland—land of my mother's ancestors. From Scotland, we trained alongside or interacted with a number of foreign special operation units: the British Special Boat Service, French Commando Hubert, German Combat Swimmers (Kampfschwimmer), Norwegian Navy Ranger Command (Marinejegerkommandoen), and others. For winter warfare training, I enjoyed over a month of fun with the Swedish Coastal Rangers (Kustjägarna), who perform long-range reconnaissance, sabotage, and assaults against enemies invading Sweden's coast. During the Cold War, Russia was their biggest threat.

I also started to hear whisperings about a Top Secret SEAL Team Six. After the 1980 failed attempt to rescue American hostages at the U.S. Embassy in Iran, the Navy asked Richard Marcinko to create a full-time counterterrorist team. As its first commanding officer, Marcinko named the new unit SEAL Team Six. He recruited heavily from the SEALs' two counterterrorist units: Mobility Six (MOB Six) at SEAL Team Two on the East Coast and Echo Platoon at SEAL Team One on the West Coast. They wore civilian clothes and longer haircuts and were allowed to grow nonregulation beards and mustaches. Officers and enlisted men addressed each other by first names and nicknames, not using military salutes. They specialized in rescuing hostages from ships, oil rigs, and other maritime locations. In addition, they assisted with military base and embassy security. On top of all that, Team Six also supported CIA operations.

While I was at SEAL Team Two, my uncle Carroll died of a heart attack while fishing. My heart ached as I returned home for the funeral. Relatives, friends, and people I didn't know packed the inside of the church. At the front, Uncle Carroll lay in his casket. He had loved me, spent time with me, and helped me grow up to be a young man. The memorial service was a blur to me—hymns, prayers, readings from the Bible, words from Brother Ron, and a eulogy. Sitting on the pew, I just physically couldn't take it. I rose to my feet and walked outside the front door of the church. I stood on the steps and cried, shaking uncontrollably. It was the hardest I had ever cried. Someone put his arms around me and hugged me. I looked up expecting to see Brother Ron, but the man with his arms around me wasn't Brother Ron. He was Dad. It was only our second hug. Not like the forced one before I got on the bus for college. "You know, Howard, I'm going to miss him, too. He always took the time with you because he was better at training you than I was. He had more patience. That's why Uncle Carroll always did that with you."

Happier news came on June 6, 1990, when my daughter, Rachel, was born. Even so, as much as I loved my new daughter, part of me was preoccupied with the Team. Maybe some SEALs can balance God, family, and the Teams. I couldn't. The Teams were everything. After staying at the hospital for a day or two, I was gone again. But whenever I returned home, she was Daddy's girl.

6.
Desert Storm

With Iraq's economy failing, President Saddam Hussein blamed Kuwait, invading the country on August 2, 1990, and taking Western hostages. The UN condemned the invasion, demanded a withdrawal, placed economic sanctions on Iraq, and formed a blockade. However, Hussein seemed poised to invade Saudi Arabia next.

On August 7, Operation Desert Shield began. Its goal was to protect Persian Gulf countries from Saddam's aggression. U.S. aircraft carriers and other ships entered the gulf. Our troops were sent to Saudi Arabia. The UN gave Iraq an ultimatum to leave Kuwait by January 15, 1991, or be forcefully removed. We formed a coalition of thirty-four countries, with financial contributions from Germany and Japan.

While my platoon readied our equipment we learned that Desert *Shield* was about to become Desert *Storm,* a military offensive against Iraq. We flew to a base on the coast of the Mediterranean Sea to meet the *John F. Kennedy,* the same aircraft carrier where I'd done Search and Rescue.

The *John F. Kennedy* was 1,052 feet long and 192 feet tall from the waterline to the top of the mast. It could sail at 34 knots (1 knot equals roughly 1.15 miles per hour) carrying more than five thousand personnel. Along with more than eighty aircraft, it was armed with two Guided Missile Launching System Mark-29 launchers for Sea Sparrow missiles, two Phalanx close-in weapon systems for attacking incoming missiles, and two Rolling Airframe Missile launchers that fire infrared homing surface-to-air missiles.

I saw a lot of my old buddies on board. Fortunately, we had a great rapport with the ship personnel. Whenever the ship's crew saw us coming through the passageway wearing our camouflage uniforms and SEAL tridents, they said, "Make a hole, SEAL coming through." It felt like being a celebrity. At first no one approached us when we were in the chow hall. After a while, people started to join us. They asked us about BUD/S and other things. In the huge hangar bay, we did our physical training every morning. Some of the ship's personnel showed up and joined us.

We didn't follow the Dick Marcinko Charm School of arrogance and alienating people. Marcinko created SEAL Team Six, served time in jail for defrauding the government, wrote his autobiography, entitled *Rogue Warrior,* and made a video game. Although I respect that he created Team Six, Marcinko gave us a black eye by disrespecting people who weren't SEALs—and by disrespecting SEALs who weren't part of his clique. I was on a flight once with a pilot who was amazed at our behavior in comparison with the loud, obnoxious, gun-waving attitude of Marcinko's SEALs. For years, we had to overcome that legacy. Especially at SEAL Team Six, subsequent commanders worked hard to clean up the crap stains Marcinko left behind.

On the *John F. Kennedy,* we were visitors in someone else's home. We treated the crew well, and they treated us like royalty.

For over a week, pilots from our ship took off loaded up with bombs, leaving us behind to watch their payloads explode on CNN. *We're missing out.* My platoon and I weren't the only ones. Although

General Norman Schwarzkopf had used British special ops, the Special Air Service (SAS), at the beginning of the war, he didn't use American special ops. He clearly favored American conventional forces over American unconventional units like the SEALs or Delta. It sucked.

On a side note, although the SEALs had specifically rehearsed to protect the oil wells in Kuwait, Schwarzkopf didn't use us. Later, Saddam's troops set fire to over six hundred of Kuwait's oil wells. Kuwait lost five to six million barrels of oil each day. Unburned oil formed hundreds of oil lakes, contaminating forty million tons of earth. Sand mixed with oil created "tarcrete," covering 5 percent of Kuwait. They burned for more than eight months, polluting the ground and air throughout the eastern Arabian Peninsula. The environmental and human suffering caused by the fires continues to be felt to this day. If it hadn't been for Schwarzkopf's underestimating their ability to light fires, the belief among the Team guys was that, we could've eliminated many of the booger-eaters before they reached the wells.

One evening, we were awakened around midnight to muster in one of the jet fighter wing's ready rooms. Intel told us that a cargo ship disguised under an Egyptian flag was laying mines in the Red Sea. Our mission would be to take the ship down.

We started our mission planning. How many helicopters? Who's going to be in what bird? Who's going to be in what seat? Which helicopter will hover over the ship first? Which helo is second? How will we set up sniper positions? Escape and evasion plans if we have to bail? Meanwhile we continued to get new intelligence, and the aircraft carrier moved us closer to striking position. We went to the intelligence center to update our intel and check out blueprints of the cargo ship we'd take down. How many decks? How many rooms? How many crew members? The amount of intel and planning that goes into a mission is mind-boggling.

We geared up, wearing black BDUs (Battle Dress Uniforms—the name for the military's former combat uniforms). On our feet, we wore Adidas GSG9 assault boots. They're soft on the bottom and grip well, like wearing a tennis shoe with ankle support. You can get them wet and fins slip on easy over the tops. To this day, that's my favorite boot. Black balaclavas covered our heads, and paint covered our exposed skin. For our hands, we customized our green aviator gloves by dying them black, then cutting off two of the fingers on the right-hand glove: the trigger finger down to the second knuckle and the thumb down to the first knuckle. With the fingers cut out, it became easier to squeeze the trigger, change magazines, pull the pins on flashbangs, etc. Casio watches on our wrists kept time. On my belt, in the small of my back, sat a gas mask. During Desert Storm, everyone prepared for gas or biological weapons. Hussein was reported to still have chemical weapons that he wouldn't hesitate to use. I also took along two or three flashbangs.

I carried the Heckler and Koch MP-5 submachine gun with a SIG SAUER 9 mm on my right hip. I kept a thirty-round magazine in the MP-5. Some guys like to carry two magazines in the weapon, but our experience was that the double magazine limited our maneuverability, and it's hard to do a magazine change. I carried three magazines on my left thigh and an extra three in my backpack. We test-fired our weapons off the fantail, on the back of the ship.

Although we had sixteen guys in our platoon, one would remain as a sniper in each of the two circling helicopters. That left only fourteen of us to take down the entire ship—two more helos with seven assaulters in each. Mine would be the lead helicopter.

We approached the ship from the rear. As we leveled out to a hover over the ship, I had enough daylight left to see the deck. We were in position. I kicked the 90-foot rope out the door and called, "Rope!" It hit the fantail on an area too small to land a helicopter.

"Go!" Wearing thick wool inserts in my gloves, I grabbed the rope and slid down it like a fireman's pole. With more than 100 pounds of gear on my back, I had to grip the rope tight to prevent myself from splattering onto the deck. My gloves literally smoked on the way down. Fortunately, I landed safely.

Unfortunately, our pilot had a hard time holding his position over the ship in rough seas with darkness falling and gusts of wind blowing. To add to the difficulty, the pilots weren't used to hovering over a target while a 200-pound man and his 100 pounds of gear come off the rope—causing the helo to suddenly gain altitude. The pilot would have to compensate by lowering the helo for each man who dismounted the rope. We had practiced with the pilots earlier, but it was still a tricky maneuver. Without the pilot's compensation, the first operator would slide off the rope with three feet of extra rope on the deck, the second guy with only a foot, and the third guy with the rope not quite reaching the deck—it wouldn't take long before some poor bastard dropped ten feet through the air with nothing to hold on to, the metal deck giving a lot less cushion than dirt. Even for the more experienced Black Hawk pilots, it's a tricky maneuver.

The helicopter pulled away. It would have to circle around, reestablish visual, make another approach, and hover again. *Crap.* There I was, in the middle of a war, in the middle of the Red Sea, on a strange enemy ship by myself. I felt naked. *If this goes really bad, I can fight my way through it. If this goes really, really bad— Mother Ocean is right there. Kick, stroke, and glide.* It probably only took two minutes for the helicopter to return, but it felt like two hours.

I scanned the area with the muzzle of my MP-5 while my platoon fast-roped down. Once we were all together, we set our perimeter. Mark, who was our team leader, and DJ, our communications (coms) guy, took a group to the wheelhouse for command and control. Two shooters went to after steering to disable the ship—making it dead in the water. My team went to the cabins to get the crew.

Inside the ship, we approached the first cabin. SEALs have a saying: "You're soft until you're hard." Stay quiet for as long as possible. If I'd heard a shot or a flashbang, I'd be thinking, *Aw, crap. Here we go.* From then on out I'd be hard. Kick in every door and flashbang every room. Manhandle everyone. Violence of action turns up exponentially. We try to match the level of violence to the level required for the situation. No more, no less.

I opened the door, and four of us slipped in quietly while two stayed behind in the hallway to cover our rear. Speed is key, as is moving together. Two of us cleared left and two cleared right. The two crew members inside froze. We dominated the area. They couldn't speak English, but we knew some Arabic: *Down.*

They assumed the position.

Another SEAL and I stood next to the wall covering while two SEALs said, "Moving."

"Move," I answered, controlling the room.

They cuffed the two crew members on the deck.

I shouted, requesting to know if the hall outside was secure for us to come out. "Coming out?"

"Come out," came a reply from the hall.

We took our prisoners out into the hallway and moved on to the next door. Most rooms averaged two crew members. Some rooms were empty.

In one room, we went in and cuffed the crew. I said, "Coming out?"

"No," the two shooters in the hall replied.

The four of us stayed put with our two prisoners—waiting. I could hear arguing in the hall.

"Wasdin," one of the guys in the hall called.

I stepped into the hallway and saw a crew member standing in a T-intersection at the end of the hall. In his hand was a fire extinguisher. One of our shooters was about to cap him for noncompliance.

"What's going on?" I asked.

"This guy won't listen," the shooter said.

Maybe he thinks we're sabotaging the ship. "Down," I said in Arabic.

The crew member spoke Arabic. "No."

I looked in his eyes. He seemed confused, not like he was being hostile for the sake of being hostile. Thinking it was simple miscommunication, I lowered my MP-5 submachine gun a little.

He lunged at me with his fire extinguisher.

Damn.

I sidestepped just as the fire extinguisher glanced off the side of my head. Back then, we weren't wearing assault helmets. If I hadn't sidestepped, the blow would've caught me straight in the face.

Wow. He almost killed me with a fire extinguisher. How would that look? Try to be nice and get taken out with a fire extinguisher. I was furious. I caught him sideways and buried the muzzle of my MP-5 under his right ear, pushed him back, then gave him a butt stroke for good measure.

One of Mr. Fire Extinguisher's buddies, a skinny little man, put up his hands as if to take me on.

My Teammate was about to cap him.

"No, I got it." With my left hand, I gave Fire Extinguisher's buddy a karate chop just below his nose, backing him off. I put enough force into it that he probably needed to get his teeth re-tightened. He quickly became compliant, not wanting any more.

Then Fire Extinguisher got cuffed the *hard* way: arm bar, knee behind the neck, grabbing a handful of his hair, lifting him up by the cuffs until his arms almost came out of their sockets, and kicking him in the ass down the hallway. Our guys took him and the other prisoners to the holding area.

Blood trickled from my head down into my ear. Now I was really pissed. *Try to be a nice guy, and that's what happens.* In retrospect, Fire Extinguisher should've gotten two to the body and one to the head. He's a lucky sonofabitch.

We found most of the men in the crew's quarters, which doubled as a chow hall—interrupting their Turkish tea and cigarettes.

We cleared nearly every inch of the ship, top to bottom, stern to bow. SEAL Team Six would take the same ship down with thirty assaulters. Since we had fewer guys and were not as specialized as Six, it took us two hours. My team stayed on the bow with the prisoners in the darkness. Mark commanded our platoon from the wheelhouse while DJ ran coms next to him.

Nobody got hurt. Other than me being an idiot.

Now the ship belonged to us. Warships surrounded us as we sat dead in the water. Rigid Hull Inflatable Boats (RHIBs) floated beside us carrying Coast Guard Law Enforcement Detachment (LEDET), the lead agency for apprehending drug traffickers on the high seas. To a large degree, the dangerous part was over.

We mustered the prisoners. The ship's captain, up in the wheelhouse with Mark, sent his master-at-arms down to do a head count. We found out we were missing one of the ship's crew. *Somebody's hiding.*

We asked the prisoners if they knew where he was.

Nobody knew nothin'.

So we had to clear the whole freaking ship again. Leaving four men to guard the prisoners, we went back to after steering and started over. We were beyond pissed, tearing through every inch of the ship we thought we'd already searched. Halfway through clearing the ship, I got a call that we'd found the guy. He had been hiding tucked up between some pipes in an engine compartment, scared.

We took him to join his comrades on the bow, and we cut the flexicuffs off all the prisoners. Except Fire Extinguisher. I made him sit on the capstan, which looks like a giant motorized thread spool, the most uncomfortable seat on the bow.

Meanwhile, Mark spoke through DJ to an interpreter on one of the ships in order to communicate to the captain standing next to Mark.

"Were you laying mines? Where were the mines? Where are you going? Where are you coming from?"

The captain and crew still weren't giving us the right answers, so LEDET, armed with shotguns, came aboard and high-fived us, and we turned over the ship and prisoners to them. They would sail the ship to a friendly port in the Red Sea, where it wouldn't be the end of the story for the prisoners by any means.

Fire Extinguisher still had his cuffs on as LEDET took over. I hope he still has them on to this day. We boarded the amphibious ship in the early morning, having been awake for more than twenty-four hours. Later I would receive the Navy Commendation Medal, which read:

> The Secretary of the Navy takes pleasure in presenting the Navy Commendation Medal to Hull Technician First Class Howard E. Wasdin, United States Navy, for services set forth in the following citation: For professional achievement and superior performance of his duties while serving as air operations specialist for SEAL Team Two Foxtrot Platoon while deployed to the Red Sea in support of Operation

Desert Storm from 17 January to 28 February 1991. During this period, Petty Officer Wasdin consistently performed his demanding duties in an exemplary and highly professional manner. As the air operations specialist responsible for all SEAL helo fast-rope operations his consistent hard work was instrumental in maintaining the assault team's capability to conduct rapid and efficient insertions onto designated targets. During one SEAL mission, he expertly directed the insertion and was the first man on deck to provide critical cover for his shipmates. He continued as lead member of a prisoner securing element displaying superior war fighting skills which proved critical to mission success. Petty Officer Wasdin's exceptional professional ability, initiative, and loyal devotion to duty reflect great credit upon himself and the United States Naval Service.

Some missions were secret. "I've been asked to select three men for a classified op, but Intel won't tell me what it's about until I select the men," Mark said one day. I didn't need to know before saying yes.

DJ and I and my friend and teammate Smudge joined him inside the Carrier Intelligence Center (CVIC), an office on the ship. In the middle of the room stood the ship's intelligence officer. Beside him was a man we'd never seen before. I didn't know if he was a spy or what. Without identifying himself, the man said, "Morning, gentlemen."

"Good morning, sir." We didn't know his rank, but it was safer to be overly polite than disrespectful.

"A Tomahawk missile was fired that missed its target and did not detonate. It landed in friendly territory, but there are enemy forces in the area. We need you to detonate the missile so the Iraqis cannot get the technology, which is invaluable. Also, we don't want them converting the explosives into an IED [Improvised Explosive Device]."

We returned to the berthing, where our beds (racks), lockers, and a small lounge were located, and began gearing up. I'd be using my CAR-15, which had a telescopic buttstock and held thirty rounds of .223 (5.56 mm) ammo in the magazine. Inside the stock, I put a few hundred dollars. In my left thigh cargo pocket, I stuck my E&E (Escape and Evasion) kit: pencil flare, waterproof matches, compass, map, red-lens flashlight, space blanket, and MRE entrée. Into the right thigh cargo pocket went my blowout (medical) kit: 4" × 4" gauze bandage with tie straps, a cravat, and a Vaseline-coated dressing for a sucking chest wound—all vacuum sealed in plastic to be waterproof. This was a minimum kit, mainly for a gunshot wound/bleeding trauma. Although SEALs often dress differently and carry a variety of weapons, the location of our blowout kit is universal. This way, if one of our shooters goes down, we don't have to play a guessing game of where his kit is to patch him up. Of course, I could use my own blowout kit to patch up an injured Teammate, but later if the need arose for me to patch myself up, I would lack the materials to do it.

The four of us boarded the SH-3 Sea King, light brown and sand-colored stripes and blotches painted on our faces. Smudge carried 4 pounds of the off-white colored modeling clay with a slight odor of hot asphalt—C-4 plastic explosives. I carried the blasting caps, fuse, and fuse igniters. The C-4 couldn't blow up without the smaller explosion of a blasting cap, which is why we separated the two. Smudge had the safer cargo. Although blasting caps alone aren't powerful enough to blow off a hand, they have been known to blow off a careless finger or two.

We traveled light because this would be a quick in-and-out. The helo flew a few miles before slowing down to 10 knots, 10 feet above the water. I stepped out the side of the bird with my swim fins pointed straight down, falling through the stinging ocean spray kicked up by the helicopter. I couldn't hear my splash over the sound of the rotor blades chopping the air overhead.

One by one, the guys jumped out the side door and into the ocean. Similar to fast-roping, when each man jumped, it lightened the helicopter's load, making the helo gain altitude—the pilot had to compensate. The last SEAL to die in Vietnam, Lieutenant Spence Dry, was doing a helo cast when the helo rose significantly higher than 20 feet while flying faster than 20 knots—breaking Dry's neck.

Treading water, I looked around. Everyone seemed to be in one piece. A light blinked from the shore—our signal. I started to feel cold. We formed a line and faced the signal. Swimming the sidestroke, I kicked long, deep, and slow, propelling myself quickly, trying to stay in formation with the others. The swim warmed me. As we reached water shallow enough to stand in, we stopped, watching the shore. No danger signs yet. I removed my fins and hooked them to a bungee cord strapped across my back. Then we slithered onto the beach. Smudge and DJ spread out to the left and right flanks. I covered Mark with my CAR-15 as he approached the light source, a pear-shaped Arab who was our agent. They exchanged silent passwords. Mark pulled his left ear. The agent rubbed his stomach with his left hand. *So far, so good.* Turning the agent with his back to me, I cuffed him and searched his body for a weapon, a radio, or anything that didn't belong. Nothing seemed out of place. I cut off his cuffs.

We drove twenty minutes into the desert and found the missile. Smudge prepared the C-4.

I added the blasting caps and fuse ignites. *Pop!* "Fire in the hole." I could smell the cordite of the fuses burning. Before the big explosion, there would be a three-minute time delay, give or take a few seconds.

We took cover behind a natural berm that looked like a giant speed bump. *Kaboom!* Sand rained down on us.

We returned to the missile, making sure it was in small enough pieces. Mark gave the OK signal.

We returned to the beach, unbungeed our fins, and entered the water to meet the helo offshore. After we'd all climbed safely onto it, we slapped each other on the back and breathed easy.

A few days later, I stood outside the CVIC again with DJ. Mark called us in and, once again, we met the Man with No Name.

He shook our hands and wasted no time. "Shall we get to it?"

We nodded.

He explained, "The Palestine Liberation Organization voiced support for Saddam Hussein's invasion of Kuwait. Now they have set up shop in Iraq. The Iranians are working with the PLO to train terrorists to attack coalition forces. Recently, they planted a roadside IED that hit one of our vehicles. We want you to target the PLO-Iranian compound in Southeastern Iraq for a guided missile strike, then report a BDA [battle damage assessment]."

Mark discussed his plan with us, and then DJ and I went off to prepare our gear. As always, we made sure we had nothing shiny or noisy on us—nothing that a little sand-colored spray paint or tape couldn't fix. After prepping our gear, we took a late-afternoon flight on a Sea King from the *John F. Kennedy*'s flight deck. I fell asleep during the flight and woke up when we landed at the forward operating base. The sky had become dark—time was ticking. A civilian named Tom with a plain face who wore blue jeans and a gray T-shirt handed us the keys to a Humvee. "I just had her washed and waxed."

I looked at the dirty vehicle and smiled. *Perfect.*

With no clouds and a half moon overhead, DJ and I could see in the darkness. So could the enemy, but the clear skies would help the missile find its target. After driving 30 miles through the desert avoiding roads, buildings, populated areas, and telephone poles, we arrived in an area where the ground gently dipped 10 feet, just as we had seen on the satellite map in the CVIC. After creating false tracks past our location, we stopped in the dip and blotted out our real insertion tracks. Next, we covered the vehicle with desert camouflage netting. We lay on the ground next to each other, facing opposite directions. Quietly we watched and listened to find out if anyone would visit us. The first few minutes were maddening. *Is that really a bush? Maybe they're watching us. How many of them are there? Will the Humvee start up again if we need to bug out? Will we be able to get away fast enough?* Thirty minutes later, I calmed down, and we moved forward on foot, using a GPS for navigation.

With only two of us, we had less firepower than a boat crew and exercised additional caution not to be seen. Our ears became sharply tuned to the slightest sounds. We crouched as we walked—slow and silent, avoiding high ground that might cause our silhouettes to stand out.

Three miles later, we reached the base of a hill. The PLO-Iranian compound lay on the other side. I walked point with DJ behind me, and we climbed nearly 600 feet until we neared a slope. Keeping the slope below us and the ridge above, we low-crawled around toward the other side of the hill. A mile ahead on the ground, I saw the wall of a compound form a triangle with guard towers in each corner surrounding three buildings inside. I also saw an enemy soldier sitting about 60 yards away to the right of our hill with binoculars around his neck and an AK-47 assault rifle slung over the back of his right shoulder.

I stopped and signaled DJ with a clenched fist: *Freeze.* DJ stopped.

The sentry remained still.

After pointing two fingers to my eyes, then in the direction of the enemy sentry, I crawled in reverse. DJ backed out, too. We stalked around the back of the hill until we found another slope. This time when we crossed over, we had a clear view of the target with no sentries nearby. Our eyes searched the immediate area around us, then farther out until the compound came into view. The only people visible were the guards in the towers.

While I guarded the perimeter, DJ sent an encrypted transmission burst over his radio to tell the USS *San Jacinto* we were in position. A burst message must've come back, because DJ nodded his head, giving me the green light.

I unpacked the lightweight laser designator (AN/PED-1 LLDR), which wasn't very lightweight, while DJ covered our perimeter. After marking our position with a beacon, I aimed at the middle building in the PLO-Iranian compound, marking it with coded pulses of invisible laser light. The light would sparkle off the target and into the sky for the incoming Tomahawk missile to find.

The cruise missile seemed to fly parallel to the earth. A trail of white smoke followed its flaming tail. The Tomahawk gradually descended until it shot into the center building, and 1,000 pounds of explosives burst in a ball of flame followed by clouds of black smoke. The shock wave and debris ripped apart the two other buildings and walls, causing a secondary detonation in one building—probably housing explosives used in making IEDs. Two of the three guard towers were ripped off. Through my binoculars, I clearly saw a soldier blasted out of his tower and sailing through the air like a stuffed doll. Only remnants remained of the compound wall. I could see no movement coming from the compound. From our hill the sentry ran toward the compound, probably hoping to find survivors among his friends.

We packed up and moved out, taking a different path to our vehicle. It's easy to become complacent on the way home, so it's important to be extra cautious. After removing the camouflage netting, we hopped in and drove away. Again we drove back a different route than we came in.

During the drive back, I noticed what appeared to be an enemy bunker, halfway exposed out of the ground. As I drove around to avoid it, the Humvee bogged down in the sand. When I tried to drive out, the Humvee wheels dug deeper, making the situation worse.

Meanwhile, Iraqi soldiers exited the bunker.

DJ and I aimed our CAR-15s at them.

Fourteen of them walked toward us with their hands in the air. I saw no threat in their faces. They were dirty and stank. Their skin stretched tight over their bones; there was no telling how long they'd been without food. They put their hands to their mouths, the international gesture for food. We'd heard some Iraqis had actually surrendered to camera crews, they were so willing to surrender and unwilling to fight.

On the ground, rags stuck from the ends of their rifles to keep the sand out. We stepped out of our vehicle and told them to dig a hole with their hands. Next we ordered them to toss in their weapons. As they did, they seemed more frightened, as if they expected us to execute them. We motioned for them to cover the hole. Their fear subsiding, they complied. Some of them probably had wives. Kids. Most of them were around my age. Their lives were totally in my hands. They looked at me like I was Zeus coming down from Mount Olympus.

Feeling sorry for them, I took out two MREs that I had broken down as emergency rations for escape and evasion. For fourteen guys, that wasn't a lot of food, but they split the two meals up among themselves. One guy even ate the Chiclets. *Well, you know, that's really candy-coated chewing gum, but go ahead. Knock yourself out.* We gave them most of our water. They put their hands together and bowed with gratitude, thanking us. Wisely, they didn't try to touch us or get in our personal space.

The faint glow of the sun began to appear on the horizon. Time to move. We made them put their hands on their heads. I marked the position of our Humvee on the GPS and walked the point while DJ followed at rear security. We looked like the gods of war. *Two Navy SEALs capture fourteen Iraqi soldiers.*

When we reached the base, Tom's response was, "Why in the hell are you giving us these guys?"

"Well, what did you want us to do with them?"

"Keep them."

"We can't keep them."

Soon our helicopter arrived, and we left our prisoners there, still bowing with their hands together and thanking us. The helo lifted off and took us back to the *John F. Kennedy.*

Through my training and service up to then, I had been in the mindset that everyone I went up against was a bad guy. *We* were morally superior to *them.* I used language to make killing more respectable: *"waste," "eliminate," "remove," "dispatch," "dispose"* . . . In the military, bombings are "clean surgical strikes" and civilian deaths are "collateral damage." Following orders takes the responsibility of killing off my shoulders and places it on a higher authority. When I bombed the compound, I further diffused personal responsibility by sharing the task: I painted the target, DJ radioed the ship, and someone else pressed the button that launched the missile. It's not uncommon for combat soldiers to dehumanize the enemy—Iraqis become "ragheads" and "camel jockeys." In the culture of war, the line between victim and aggressor can become blurred. All these things helped me do my job, but they also threatened to blind me to the humanity in my enemy.

Of course, SEALs train to match the appropriate level of violence required by the situation, turning it up and down like the dimmer on a light switch. You don't always want the chandeliers on bright. Sometimes you do. That switch is inside me still. I don't want to, but I can turn it on if needed. However, the training didn't prepare me for seeing the humanity in those fourteen men. It's something you have to be in real combat to see. Not simulated combat. Maybe I could've put a bullet in every one of their skulls and bragged about how many confirmed kills I got. Some people have this idea of SEALs just being mindless, wind-me-up killing machines. "Oh, you're an assassin." I don't like that. I don't adhere to it. Most SEALs know that if you can do an op without any loss of life, it's a great op.

Seeing those fourteen men, I realized they were not bad guys. They were just poor sonsofbitches who were half starved to death, underequipped, outgunned, having no clue, and following some madman who'd decided he wanted to invade another country. If they didn't follow the madman, the Republican Guard would execute them. I suspect they lost the will to fight. Maybe they never had the will to fight in the first place.

They were human beings just like me. I discovered my humanity and the humanity in others. It was a turning point for me—it was when I matured. My standards of right and wrong in combat became clearer, defined by what I did and didn't do. I did give the fourteen Iraqi soldiers food and take them to a safer place. I didn't kill them. Whether you're winning or losing, war is hell. It's important to understand that our enemies are human.

Desert Storm only lasted forty-three days. We were furious that we didn't go to Baghdad and finish it. The *Kennedy* stopped in

Egypt, where we checked into a five-star resort in Hurghada. Not being tourist season, and with the recent war, we were the only guests. During dinner, our platoon chief came in and slapped me on the back. "Congratulations, Wasdin, you made First Class." Life was pretty good for Howard.

I didn't have flashbacks, nightmares, trouble sleeping, impaired concentration, depression, or self-devaluation about having killed for the first time—seeing the soldier blasted out of the PLO guard tower and landing lifeless on the ground. Those kinds of feelings seem less common among special ops guys. Maybe most of the people susceptible to that stress were already weeded out during BUD/S, and maybe the high levels of stress in our training prepare us for the high levels of stress in war. I began to control my thoughts, emotions, and pain at an early age—it was a matter of survival—which helped me cope with challenges in the Teams. I had endured the trauma of my dad's harshness, Hell Week, and other experiences, and I endured war.

I did have a moral concern about having killed for the first time, though. I was worried whether I'd done the right thing. On TV and video games, it may seem like killing is no big deal. However, I had made the decision to end someone's life. The people I killed will never see their families again. Will never eat or use the restroom again. Never breathe again. I took everything that they had or ever will have. To me, that was a big deal. Something I didn't take lightly. Even now, I still don't take it lightly. During a visit home, I talked to Brother Ron. "I killed in combat for the first time. Did I do the right thing?"

"You lawfully served your country."

"How is this going to affect me as far as eternity goes?"

"It won't have a negative affect on your eternity."

His words comforted me. My youngest sister, Sue Anne, who is a therapist, is convinced that I've got to have something wrong with me. There's no way I'm functioning as normally as I am without repressing something. She just doesn't get the fact that I really am OK with my decisions and mental peace.

Smudge, DJ, four other SEALs from Foxtrot Platoon, and I handed in our applications for joining SEAL Team Six. Smudge, DJ, and I passed the application stage, but the others didn't. One guy was extremely pissed because he'd been a SEAL longer than I had.

I underwent the main screening in Dam Neck, Virginia. SEALs were lined up for interviews like kids at Disneyland anxiously waiting for a ride on Space Mountain. Guys like us had flown in from Scotland. Others flew in from California, Puerto Rico, the Philippines, and other places. For some, this wasn't the first time they'd interviewed.

Six usually required applicants to have been SEALs for five years. If I hadn't been a player in Desert Storm, I probably would've had to wait another two and a half years.

Two weeks later, Skipper Norm Carley called Smudge, DJ, and me into his office. He gave us our date to start "Green Team," the selection and training process to become a SEAL Team Six operator. "Congratulations. I hate to see you men go, but you're going to have a blast at SEAL Team Six."

PART TWO

It's a whole lot better to go up the river with seven studs than a hundred s***heads.

—Colonel Charlie A. Beckwith,
U.S. ARMY DELTA FORCE FOUNDER

7.
SEAL Team Six

Most of us were in our thirties. I was exactly thirty. Despite our experience, Green Team was meant to cut a few of us. The instructors evaluated us and ranked everything we did, including our runs and swims. We had scores and rankings for everything.

We practiced land warfare, parachuting, and diving—all taken to a whole new level. For example, we probably did around a hundred and fifty parachute jumps within four weeks: free-falling, HAHO (High Altitude, High Opening), canopy stacking (lining up in mid-air during the parachute descent), etc. Our curriculum included free-climbing, unarmed combat, defensive and offensive driving, and Survival, Evasion, Resistance, and Escape (SERE). Although we spent a little time on skills such as how to break into a car and how to start it with a screwdriver, we spent more time on how to maneuver the vehicle and shoot from it. More than learning how to pick a lock open, we learned how to blow the door off its hinges. We shot thousands of rounds every day. I was told that in one year, SEAL Team Six alone spent more money just on 9 mm ammunition than the entire Marine Corps spent on all its ammunition.

I learned close-quarters combat at a whole new level. Even though I was already a SEAL, I hadn't done it like SEAL Team Six does it. During one drill, we had to enter a room, engage the targets, shuffle-shoot, sprint, and shoot a stop target. The instructors constantly reconfigured the rooms: big, small, square, rectangle, enemy, friendly. They constantly reconfigured the furniture inside the rooms, too. We were constantly under scrutiny; the instructors showed us recordings of our performance on video.

Bobby Z., a tall blond-haired kid, and I were always within a couple of seconds of each other. Sometimes we were so close that I felt the blast of his muzzle blow my hair—this was with live ammo. A large gap grew between us and everyone else. After reviewing the video, we saw that Bobby and I didn't slow down while we shuffle-shot side to side. Most people slow down a lot to engage their targets, but we didn't. Bobby kicked my butt on the runs and swims.

While in Green Team, Bobby and I went back and forth in the number one position. I ended up being ranked at number two. Part of the reason for the ranking was that we actually went through a draft. Scouts from three units within SEAL Team Six—Red, Blue, and Gold Teams—came out to watch us train. Each of them wanted to take the best.

SEALs constantly work in danger, but Team Six pushed those danger levels higher. In the first years of Six's formation, during CQC training, a Team member stumbled and accidentally squeezed the trigger, shooting Roger Cheuy in the back. Cheuy later died in the hospital due to a staph infection. "Staph" is short for "staphylococcal," and that strain of bacteria produces toxins similar to those in food poisoning. The Team member was not only kicked out of Six but kicked out of the SEALs. In another incident, a freak CQC accident, a bullet went through one of the partitions in the kill house and entered between the joints in Rich Horn's bullet-resistant vest, killing him. In a parachuting mishap, Gary Hershey died, too.

Six months after my Green Team started, four or five men had failed out of thirty. Although we had some injuries, none of them were fatal. Red, Blue, and Gold made their first picks of the draft. Red Team picked me up in the first round. Just like the NFL draft. Similar to the Washington Redskins, Red Team's logo was the American Indian—some activists may find it offensive, but we embraced the bravery and fighting skills of the Indians.

Just because I got drafted in the first round didn't mean I got treated better in the Team. I became an assault member just like everybody else. My boat crew was one of four. I was still the new guy. Never mind I'd been in combat and some of them hadn't. I would have to earn their respect.

Now I belonged to a cover organization with an official commander, address, and secretary to answer the phone. When applying for a credit card, I couldn't very well tell them I worked for SEAL Team Six. Instead, I gave them the information for my cover organization. I showed up to work in civilian clothes, rather than a uniform. Nobody breathed the words "SEAL Team Six" back then.

Even after passing Green Team and gaining acceptance to Team Six, we continued to hone our skills. For shooting, we went to John Shaw's Mid-South Institute of Self-Defense Shooting in Lake Cormorant, Mississippi. He had a huge range with left-to-right, pop-up, and other targets. His kill house was top of the line. Eight of us from Red Team went there to train. That was exactly the kind of opportunity that had made me want to join SEAL Team Six in the first place.

In spite of being the new guy, I had my eyes on the next challenge: becoming a sniper. I was an adrenaline junkie for sure. SEAL Team Six wanted us to be in our individual color teams for three years before applying to become a sniper.

During the fall of 1992, I requested to go to sniper school. Our

Red Team chief, Denny Chalker, told me, "You're a great opera-tor, but you haven't been in the Team long enough. It's an unwrit-ten rule that we want you here three years before you go to sniper school. Besides, your boat crew leader doesn't want to lose you."

Red Team only had two snipers, though, and we needed four to six. My being a hell of a shot didn't hurt matters. A week later, Denny said, "You know what? We changed our mind—you can do it. We're going to send you and Casanova to sniper school."

Although we would stay in Red Team, we would also become members of Black Team—the snipers. For training we went to the Marine Corps' Scout Sniper School at Quantico, Virginia. I knew it would be the biggest kick in the nuts—like a mini BUD/S Training—but it had the longest tradition, the most prestige, and, more important, the best reputation in the world. Among the few accepted to the school, only around 50 percent pass.

The ten-week course included three phases. On day one of Phase One, Marksman and Basic Fields Craft, we took the Physical Fit-ness Test (PFT), checked in our gear, and handed in our paper-work. Those who failed the PFT were sent home with no second chance.

The rest of us took our seats inside a cinder-block building with blacked-out windows and one classroom, called the schoolhouse, and received a general briefing about the course.

The next day, a gunny sergeant stood in front of us in the schoolhouse. He looked to be in his early forties with a marine high-and-tight haircut. He was a member of the President's Hun-dred, the top one hundred civilian and military marksmen in the yearly President's Match pistol and rifle competition. Our instruc-tors also included combat veterans and laid-back gurus, cadre of the highest caliber.

"A sniper has two missions," the gunny sergeant said. "The first is to support combat operations by delivering precision fire on selected targets from concealed positions. The sniper doesn't just go out there shooting any target—he takes out the targets that will help win the battle: officers, noncommissioned officers, scouts, crew-served weapons personnel, tank commanders, communication personnel, and other snipers. His second mission, which will take up much of the sniper's time, is observation. Gathering information."

Out on the range, Casanova and I worked together, alternating between spotter and shooter. For rifles, we had to use the Marine Corps M-40, a Remington 700 bolt-action .308 caliber (7.62×51 mm) heavy-barrel rifle that holds five rounds. Mounted on the rifle was a Unertl 10-power sniper scope. I would shoot first, so I made sure the scope was focused. Then I adjusted the bullet drop compensator on my scope to modify for the effect of gravity on the bullet before it reached its target 300 yards away. If I changed distances, I would have to correct my dope again.

Casanova looked through his M-49 20-power spotting scope, mounted on a tripod. Without the tripod, the scope's strong magnification causes the visual to shake with the slightest hand movements. Casanova used the scope to approximate wind speed, which is usually a sniper's greatest weather challenge.

Wind flags can be used to estimate wind speed by their angle. If a flag is at an 80-degree angle, that number is divided by the constant 4—to get 20 miles per hour. Likewise, if the flag only waves at a 40-degree angle, 40 divided by 4 equals 10 miles per hour.

If no flag is available, the sniper can use his observation skills. A wind that is barely felt but causes smoke to drift is less than 3 miles per hour. Light winds are 3 to 5 miles per hour. Wind that constantly blows leaves around is 5 to 8 miles per hour. Dust and trash are blown at 8 to 12 miles per hour. Trees sway at 12 to 15 miles per hour.

A sniper could also use the spotting scope method. When the sun heats the earth, the air near the surface ripples in waves. The wind causes these waves to move in its direction. To see the waves, the sniper focuses on an object near the target. Rotating the eyepiece a quarter turn counterclockwise, he focuses on the area in front of the target area, which makes the heat waves become visible. Slow wind causes big waves, while fast wind flattens them out. This method of recognizing wind speed takes practice.

Winds blowing directly from left to right, or right to left, have the most effect on a shot. They are called full value winds. Oblique winds from left to right, or right to left, are designated as half value winds. Front to rear, or rear to front, are no value winds—having the least effect.

Casanova gave me the wind speed: "Five miles per hour, full value, left to right." Three-(hundred)-yard range times 5 miles per hour equals 15; 15 divided by the constant 15 equals 1. I adjusted the horizontal reticle in my scope one click to the left. If I had two windage from the right, I'd adjust two clicks to the right.

I took my first shot at a stationary target—hit. After two more shots at stationary targets and two at moving targets, I became spotter while Casanova shot. Then we threw on our packs, grabbed our equipment, and ran back to the 500-yard line. As in the Teams, it paid to be a winner. Again, we alternated between taking five shots each at three stationary and two moving targets. Then we did the same at 600 yards. It's tough to slow the breathing and heart rate down after running. At 700 yards, we hit three stationary targets again, but this time, the two movers would stop and go. At 800 yards, the two stop-and-go movers became bobbers, waving left to right and right to left. At 900 and 1,000 yards, the five targets remained stationary. Out of thirty-five rounds, twenty-eight had to hit the black. We lost a lot of guys on the range. They just couldn't shoot well enough.

After the range, we returned to the schoolhouse and cleaned our weapons before doing a field sketch exercise. The instructors took us out to an area and said, "Draw a sketch of the area from the left wood line to the water tower on the right. You've got thirty minutes." We drew as many important details as we could, and drew in perspective: Nearby objects are larger than distant objects; horizontal parallel lines converge and vanish in the distance. On the bottom of the sketch, we wrote down what we saw: patrol, number of 2.5-ton trucks (deuce-and-a-halfs), et cetera. The instructors graded us for neatness, accuracy, and intelligence value. Seventy percent or higher was a passing grade. Later, we would only have fifteen minutes.

A sniper also keeps a log to be used with the sketch, so he has a written record of information regarding key terrain, observation, cover and concealment, obstacles, and avenue of approach (summarized as KOCOA) along with his pictorial sketch.

We also played Keep in Memory (KIM) games. The instructor would pull back a tarp on a table and expose ten to twelve small items: spent 9 mm cartridge, pencil flare, Ziploc bag, pen, broken pair of glasses, photograph of someone, acorn, and other items that could fit on the tabletop. In ten to fifteen seconds, we had to memorize everything. Then we went into the classroom, grabbed a piece of paper, and drew everything we had seen. Finally, we had to verbally describe what we saw. Sometimes we used scopes and binoculars to report full-sized items at a distance. If, on a routine basis, I couldn't remember 70 percent or more, I'd be kicked out.

In Phase Two, Unknown Distance and Stalking, those of us who remained after Phase One ran ten 100-pound steel targets out to distances between 300 and 800 yards. Because we didn't know the exact distance to the targets, we had to estimate. First-shot hits scored ten points. Second-shot hits scored eight. There were no third shots. Upon completion, Casanova and I rearranged the targets and did it again. We had to maintain a 70 percent average over the three weeks of shooting to stay in the school.

Along with shooting skills, sniper school also taught us about concealment. We had to make our own ghillie suits—camouflage clothing that looks like heavy foliage, made from loose burlap strips. First, we prepared our clothing: BDU (combat uniform) tops and bottoms. Next, using high-strength thread that wouldn't rot, such as 12-pound fishing line, we attached netting (example: a military hammock or fishing net) to the backs and elbows of our suits. Shoe Goo is even easier to use than needle and thread. Then we cut strips of burlap about 1" wide and 9" long and tied them with overhand knots onto the netting. We pulled lengthwise at the material from the end so the burlap frayed. Using a can of spray paint, we colored the burlap. Casanova and I added natural foliage from knee level or lower, which is where a sniper moves. Leaves taken from above would stand out on a sniper crawling low to the ground. We were careful not to add anything too long that might wave around like a flag. Leaves work best because they last the longest without spoiling. Grass spoils the fastest—in around four hours. Around the rifle buttstock, we wrapped an olive drab cravat and tied it off with a square knot to break up the weapon's outline. Another cravat went around the barrel and scope, similar to wrapping an arm with a bandage. Attaching burlap straps broke up the cravat's solid green color. Similarly, we camouflaged the M-49 scope, binoculars, and other gear.

On weekends, our time off, Casanova and I learned and practiced the art of invisibility. We worked on our ghillie suits. Then we wore the suits outside and lay down in different environments, trying to spot each other. Most spare hours were spent honing our invisibility skills.

Stalking caused the most students to fail. The location of each stalk varied, and we had to change our color schemes and textures to blend in. Optics came in handy during the stalk. The naked eye can scan the widest area. Binoculars can be used to take a closer look, yet maintain a relatively wide field of vision. The sniper scope usually allows a slightly closer inspection than the binoculars, but with a narrower field of vision. The spotting scope magnifies the greatest, allowing the sniper to investigate objects closely; however, the field of view is the narrowest.

The closer a sniper gets to the target, the more slowly he moves. At 2 miles to a target, the sniper stalks smoothly and quickly from cover to cover for a mile. He becomes stealthier for the next half mile, adjusting to how much cover and concealment the terrain provides. Within the last half mile to the target, the sniper's movement becomes painstakingly careful—crawling low to the ground. The right hand only moves forward one foot in thirty seconds. Then the left hand moves forward just as slowly.

Sometimes previous stalkers leave a trail. The advantage of using their trail is that they already smashed down vegetation, saving precious seconds of easing each bush or blade of grass down.

Within three to four hours, we had to stalk a distance of 800 to 1,200 yards, arriving within 200 yards of the Observer in an OP. If the Observer spotted us with his spotter scope before we got within two hundred yards of our position, we only got forty points out of one hundred—failure.

If the Observer saw a bush move, he'd call one of the Walkers on the radio. "Walker, turn left. Go three yards. Stop. Turn right. One yard. Stop. Sniper at your feet." Any sniper within a one-foot radius of the Walker was busted. Those who were busted usually hadn't made it within 200 yards of him. The sniper stood up with his gun and walked to the bus. Fifty points—failure.

Upon reaching our final firing position, within 200 yards of the Observer, we had to set up our weapon and fire a blank at the Observer. If the sniper couldn't properly ID the Observer, give correct windage or elevation, or shoot from a stable shooting platform, sixty points—failure. If we *could* do all that, but the Observer spotted the muzzle blast, he'd talk the Walker to our position and bust us. Seventy points—a minimum pass.

If the Observer didn't see the shot, the Walker shouted out to the general area where he believed the sniper to be, "Fire the second shot!"

Most people got busted because the Observer saw brush movement from the muzzle blast on the second shot. Eighty points.

The final part of the stalk was to see if the sniper could observe a signal from the Observer. If the blast of the second shot moved the medium being shot through, such as twigs, grass, or whatever, and the sniper couldn't see the Observer's signal—ninety points.

"Target is patting himself on the head," I said.

The Walker radioed the Observer, "Sniper says you're patting yourself on top of the head."

"Yep, good stalk. Stand up. Go to the bus." Perfect stalk—one hundred points. We needed at least two perfect stalks out of ten, and an overall average of 70 percent or better.

Even in fall, at 70 degrees, Quantico was still hot as hell while under the sun wearing a ghillie suit, pulling gear in a drag bag, and painstakingly creeping low on the ground. People dehydrated. After finishing the stalk, we had to go back and beat the bushes to find those who had passed out. We carried them back to the barracks.

Casanova and I stayed in a hotel room off base, while the marines stayed in the barracks across the street from sniper school. We were still on call. If our pagers went off and we had to bug out, we could leave without a lot of people wondering what was going on. Boy, we were prima donnas, having the best of everything—flying first class and renting a car for each pair of men. In our hotel room following a stalk, I had to check Casanova on the places he couldn't check himself for ticks, which might cause Lyme disease. Left untreated, Lyme disease attacks the central nervous system. Casanova did the same for me. Nothing more intimate than having your buddy use tweezers to pull a tick out from around your anus.

It took me three or four stalks before the lights went on in my brain: *Now I see what they're trying to get me to do. Keep my overhead movement down. No shine, glare, or glitter.* Some guys failed because they couldn't make their ghillie suit blend in with the environment around them.

Some guys could make their suits match the environment but couldn't stay flat. I saw so many asses in the air. Guys would crawl up next to a tree and think that the tree made them invisible. The instructors called it "tree cancer." Their eyes would follow a tree down—linear, linear, bump at the bottom. *What's that tree got—a cancerous nodule there?* Fail.

There was a lot more to sniping than just making a long-range shot. An Olympic shooter who could make the shot but couldn't make the stalk wouldn't be a sniper.

Phase Three, Advanced Field Skills and Mission Employment, included a final op. Regardless of how well we did on the shooting range, sketches, KIM games, or stalks, we had to pass the final three-day op. The instructors expected a high level of maturity and independence from us. Snipers often work in pairs without direct supervision. They must be capable of making decisions themselves, which includes decisions to adapt in a fluid environment.

Under cover of night, during the final op, Casanova and I arrived at our FFP and made our sniper hide. First, we dug down four to six inches, carefully removed the topsoil and grass, and laid it to the side. Next, we dug a pit approximately 6'×6' wide and 5' deep. At the bottom of the pit, Casanova and I dug a sump about 2' long, 1.5' wide, and 1' deep, sloped at 45 degrees to drain any rainwater or unwanted grenades. Also, to prevent the rain from caving in our hole, we lined the top rim of the pit with sandbags. Then we cleared away an area near the top of the hole where we could rest our elbows while spotting and sniping. After that, we covered our hole with logs, rain ponchos, rocks, dirt, and the sod we had placed to the side earlier. Finally, we created a rear exit hole, camouflaging it with fallen tree branches. Inside the exit hole, we placed a claymore mine to welcome any guests.

We kept a log of everything that went on at the target area, a house in the middle of nowhere with vehicles around it. A patrol walked over us but couldn't see us. At one-hour intervals, Casanova and I alternated between spotting and sniping. We ate, slept, and relieved ourselves in the hole. The hard part was keeping one of us awake while the other slept. At night, we had to get out and go take a look at the back of the house. Listening to our radio at the designated time, we received a shoot window—the time frame for taking out the target: "The man in the red hat will appear at oh two hundred on November 8. Take him out." A man with a blue hat showed up. Wrong target.

Before the op, Casanova and I prepared a range card, shaped like a protractor, of the target area. Upon arrival at our FFP, we modified it by adding details such as dominant terrain features and other objects. We divided the card into three sectors: A, B, and C. Using prearranged arm and hand signals, Casanova motioned that our target had arrived in Sector B, 1200 on a clock face, 500 yards away. Then he pointed at the location on the range card.

I acknowledged with a thumbs-up, having already dialed in my dope. My crosshairs rested on the chest of the mannequin with a red hat standing in front of a window. If I missed, I wouldn't graduate sniper school. Casanova would still get his chance to make the shot, but I would fail. I calmly squeezed the trigger. Bull's-eye. After taking the shot, we stealthily exfiltrated to our pickup point, which required land navigation with a map and compass—no GPS.

Later, dressed in our combat uniforms, we had an informal graduation.

After sniper school I returned home, but I would only have a little time to spend with my family. At work, I immediately started learning how to shoot the .300 Win Mag with the Leupold 10-power scope. Going from shooting the marine 7.62 mm sniper rifle to shooting SEAL Team Six's .300 Win Mag was like going from racing a bus to racing a Ferrari. Wind has less effect on its rounds, the trajectory is lower, the range is greater, and it has a hell of a lot more knockdown power than other rifles. For hitting a hard target, such as the engine block in a vehicle, I'd choose a .50 caliber rifle, but for a human target, the .300 Win Mag is the best. The KN-250 was our night-vision scope for the same weapon. Night vision amplifies available light from sources like the moon and stars, converting images into green and light green instead of black and white. The result lacks depth and contrast but enables the sniper to see at night.

Then we took a trip to Fort Bragg, North Carolina, and began learning how to shoot the sound-suppressed CAR-15 while strapping ourselves outside helicopters on special chairs, like bar-stool swivel chairs with backs, attached to the helo's skids. Getting up to speed on everything took a lot of time. This extended to communications—learning how to use the LST satellite radio with a special keyboard for sending encrypted burst transmissions.

Our training took us as far as Australia, to drill with the Australian Special Air Service. SEALs have a history of working with the Australian SAS that goes back to the Vietnam War.

There was a lot of respect on both sides. They taught us some stuff, and we taught them some stuff. We were all better for it—which is why exchanges are so beneficial.

In the evenings, over beers, we swapped stories. One soldier told us that he'd operated out of the same camp during the First Gulf War as the British SAS unit Bravo Two Zero, which was famous among units like ours. It was an eight-man team sent to operate in enemy territory to report enemy positions and destroy targets such as fiber-optic communication lines. During the second day of their operation, a farmer driving a bulldozer spotted them. The SAS let him go instead of detaining or killing him. Over the next few days, Bravo Two Zero survived several firefights before becoming separated. Iraqi civilian fighters killed Robert Consiglio. Vincent Phillips and Steven Lane died of hypothermia. The Iraqis captured Andy McNab, Ian Pring, Malcolm MacGown, and Mike Coburn (New Zealand SAS), who were later released. Chris Ryan evaded Iraqi troops for eight days, trekking over 200 miles to Syria, the longest escape and evasion by any soldier. During the thirty minutes of telling us the story, the SAS operator became teary-eyed, seeming to know one or more of the operators who died. His main message to us was, "If you're ever compromised, it's better to kill or tie up the person who sees you than to let him go."

8.
Born-Again Sniper

Working with foreign units like the Australian SAS was often easier than working with U.S. counterparts like Delta Force. Rivalry between U.S. units was a problem. We were about to be taught a lesson in it.

By now I was stationed at SEAL Team Six's base in Virginia Beach, Virginia. I wore my hair longer than regulations so I could blend into crowds to work. When a group of us were in public, our cover story was that we were members of a skydiving team. If people asked us about skydiving, we could answer any question. Besides, our story was too preposterous not to be real.

One night I was in a pizza place with my seven-year-old son, Blake, when my pager went off: *T-R-I-D-E-N-T-0-1-0-1*. A code could mean "Go to the SEAL Team Six compound," or tell me which base gate to use. This time, I had to go straight to the plane.

My bags would meet me on the bird. Each bag was taped up and color-coded for its specific mission. If I didn't have everything packed up correctly, I just wouldn't have it. On one op, a guy forgot the ground liner to put on the outside of his sleeping bag to keep the water from getting in. His good night's sleep wasn't very good.

During standby, we were on a one-hour leash. No matter where the heck I was, I had one hour to get my tail on the plane and sit down ready for the brief. Blake and I drove home. My wife asked, "Where you going?"

I shrugged my shoulders. "Don't know."

That was another nail in the coffin for our marriage. Who can blame her?

At the airfield I scanned the C-130. Some have jet-assisted take-off (JATO) bottles on them for taking off on short runways and getting in the air a lot quicker, a good thing to have when people are shooting at you. If I'd seen JATO bottles, I would've known our destination wasn't going to be good, but there were no JATO bottles this time. I boarded and made sure my bags were there.

Three SEAL snipers joined me: Casanova, Little Big Man, and Sourpuss. In the Teams, many of the guys went by nicknames. Casanova was the ladies' man. Little Big Man had a bad case of the small man complex, which is probably why he always carried that big-ass Randall knife on his hip. Sourpuss, the senior man, had zero personality—the one guy in the group who wasn't fun-loving. None of us really liked him.

We sat down in front of a flip chart near the cockpit. The guy giving the brief was from Joint Special Operations Command (JSOC). After the 1980 failed attempt to rescue fifty-three American hostages at the American Embassy in Iran, it became clear that the army, navy, air force, and marines couldn't work together effectively on special operations missions. In 1987, the Department of Defense grafted all the military branches' special operations onto one tree. JSOC was our boss.

Mr. JSOC was all business. Sometimes in the Teams there's a little chuckling during a brief. Now, there were no jokes. We kept our mouths shut.

He flipped the chart to an aerial photo. "OK, gentlemen, this is a TCS op."

So it wasn't a real-world op at all. It was a Task Conditions and Standards (TCS) operation. A test.

Major General William F. Garrison, JSOC commander, had thrown the BS flag on all the promises we made when we tried to win assignments. SEALs said they could do things Delta couldn't. Delta said it could do things SEALs couldn't. *Could we do what we advertised—anything, anytime, under any conditions—including an 800-yard killing shot on a human?*

That was kind of typical of Garrison. In Vietnam he earned a Bronze Star for valor and a Purple Heart for combat wounds. Later, he worked in the U.S. Army Intelligence Support Activity and in Delta. He had been the youngest general in the army—ever. Many of his men thought he was the best officer they'd ever met or would meet.

Mr. JSOC continued, "You're going to do a night HALO onto a known target." HALO meant High Altitude Low Opening: We would jump from the airplane and free-fall until we neared the ground and opened our parachutes. On a High Altitude *High* Opening (HAHO), we might jump at 28,000 feet, fall five seconds, open our chutes, and glide maybe 40 miles to the landing zone—which allowed us to avoid detection more easily.

We'd have ten minutes to take out our target. If we were late or missed the shot, we failed. No second chances. One shot, one kill.

We jumped, only pulling our ripcords after descending to 3,000 feet. I flipped on my night optical device (NOD). We each had infrared chemlight glowsticks on the backs of our helmets that were invisible to the naked eye but shone in our NODs. We steered our chutes to line up on top of each other and landed cleanly.

I took the point, leading us out. The wind blew rain at us. We patrolled a little over half a mile, then put on our ghillie suits. Casanova and I checked out each other's war paint: hands, neck, ears, and face. When painting the skin, it's important to appear the opposite of how a human being looks: Make the dark become light and the light become dark. That means making sure the parts of the face that form shadows (where the eyes sink in, etc.) become light green and the features that shine (forehead, cheeks, nose, brow, and chin) become dark green. If the sniper's face is seen, it shouldn't resemble a face.

At what we determined to be 900 yards to the target, Casanova and I lay flat on the ground and began to low-crawl. I pulled the ground with arms and pushed with my feet, face so close to the ground that it pushed mud. Six inches at a time. During stalks, I often told myself, *I am one with the ground. I am a part of this dirt.*

If I saw the target or a roving patrol, I wouldn't look directly at or think about it. Humans have a sixth sense—they know when they're being watched, some more than others. The sniper tries not to arouse this sense and avoids looking directly at the target.

At what we estimated to be 500 yards to the target, we arrived at our final firing position (FFP). Ahead of us was an old house. Casanova and I discussed range, visibility, etc. We used color codes for each side: white meant front; black meant rear; green meant the building's own right; and red meant the building's left. All the Team Six snipers used the same code so we could work with each other easily.

I mil-dotted the window—a trick for estimating the distance of object by measuring how large it appears in a sniper scope. Count how many of the crosshair dots ("mil-dots") the object covers, do a calculation based on what you know about the object's actual height, and you can have a good idea of how far away the object is. It was my job to know a typical window is one yard tall, so I only had to count the dots it covered at this distance and do some math to get the yardage. I estimated six hundred yards—a slight difference from the first estimate, but enough to make a big difference.

A figure appeared in the window—the target, which was a mannequin.

Each would only get one try—cold bore. This first shot is the worst because the round has to travel through the cold bore of the rifle. After that round warms up the barrel, the next one fires more accurately. General Garrison knew that. I heard shots from the other pair, then Casanova and I took our turns.

We carefully returned to the pickup point and flew back for debriefing—where we discovered that every one of us had missed.

One of us hadn't even shot through the window. He'd hit the windowsill. I was off in my distance estimate by more than a hundred yards.

General Garrison said, "Your sniper craft skills were remarkable. But it doesn't mean crap when all four of you miss the target! Your only hope was that the enemy might die of a heart attack from being shot at."

It turned out that the other teams had also failed. Some hadn't even made it to the target house.

Both SEALs and Delta wanted to be chosen for every mission, so we all had been promising Garrison we could do anything. The truth was we had our limits. Garrison understood that we all needed to get realistic about them. "I don't care what you can do some of the time. I want to know what you can do every time anywhere in the world under any conditions." That's what you had to love about Garrison.

All of JSOC's snipers, both SEAL and Delta operators, saw the light. We came up with what we could do every single time. That also meant learning to play together. Why should SEAL Team Six take down an aircraft on a runway when Delta does it better?

Why should Delta take down a ship when SEAL Team Six does it better? The most glaring example of this problem arose when Delta had one of several mishaps with explosives, blowing off a Delta operator's fingers. *Nobody* does explosives better than SEAL Team Six.

We had to fix this. Especially if we were going to survive one of the bloodiest battles since Vietnam—and that battle lay just around the corner.

9

CIA Safe House—
Hunting for Aidid

Less than half a year after Casanova and I finished sniper school, we received a mission: Capture the Somalian warlord Mohamed Farrah Aidid and his lieutenants. Educated in Moscow and Rome, Aidid served in the Italian colonial police force before entering the military and becoming a general of the Somalian Army. Aidid's clan (Habar Gidir), Ali Mahdi Muhammad's clan (Abgaal), and other clans overthrew Somalia's dictator. Then the two clans fought each other for control of Somalia. Twenty thousand Somalis were killed or injured, and agricultural production came to a halt. When the international community sent food, particularly the UN under Operation Restore Hope, Aidid's militia stole much of it—extorting or killing people who wouldn't cooperate—and traded the food with other countries for weapons. Starvation deaths skyrocketed to hundreds of thousands of people, and the suffering rose higher still. Although other Somali leaders tried to reach a peace agreement, Aidid would have none of it.

JUNE 5, 1993　　A Pakistani force, part of the UN humanitarian team, went to investigate an arms depot at a radio station. Aidid's people gathered outside in protest. When the Pakistanis came out of the building, the protesters attacked, killing twenty-four Pakistani soldiers. Aidid's people, including women and children, celebrated by dismembering, disemboweling, and skinning the Pakistanis. Admiral Jonathan Howe, Special Representative for Somalia to the United Nations, was horrified. He put a $25,000 warrant out on Aidid for information leading to his arrest. Howe also pushed hard for JSOC assistance.

AUGUST 8, 1993   Aidid's people used a command-detonated mine to kill four American military policemen. Enough was enough. President Bill Clinton gave JSOC the green light. The task force would include four of us from SEAL Team Six, Delta Force, Rangers, Task Force 160, and others. Task Force 160, nicknamed the "Night Stalkers," provided the helicopter support that usually operated at night, flying fast and low (to avoid radar detection). We would conduct Operation Gothic Serpent in three phases: First, deploy to Mogadishu and set up a base; Second, go after Aidid; and Third, if we didn't succeed in apprehending Aidid, go after his lieutenants.

At the Team compound in Dam Neck, Virginia, Little Big Man, Sourpuss, Casanova, and I joined in getting ready to go to Somalia: training, prepping our gear, growing beards, and letting our hair grow out. Part of prepping our gear meant going to the encryption room and coding our radios for secure voice. It was time-consuming because we had to enter a lot of codes, and they had to be the same for every handheld radio. We decided what the common frequency would be. As a sniper, I had to communicate with Casanova, my partner, and the two of us had to communicate with the other sniper pair, Little Big Man and Sourpuss. Then we all had to be able to communicate with our forward operating base. I made sure my E&E kit was complete and I had bribe/ survival cash. Then I test-fired my weapons one last time. Not knowing exactly what we'd be tasked to do, we prepared for everything. Instructors from the Defense Language Institute taught us important phrases in Somali: *stop, get down, walk backward toward my voice, hurry,* etc.

A Delta officer phoned us. "The op is on, but you won't need long hair and beards." So we got shaves and haircuts and flew back to Fort Bragg.

AUGUST 27, 1993   After eighteen hours in the air, we landed at Mogadishu Airfield within the UN compound south of Mogadishu. Egyptian peacekeepers guarded the outer perimeter. Inside the compound were peacekeeping forces from Italy, New Zealand, Romania, and Russia. West of the landing strip stood an old aircraft hangar where we would stay. Beyond the hangar stood a two-story building with a lopsided roof—the Joint Operations Center (JOC). Antennas poked out of the roof like spines on a porcupine.

We reported to General Garrison. His personal trailer had no visible family photos or knickknacks; at a moment's notice he could leave without a trace. Garrison took one look at the four of us and said, "Hey, how come you all got your hair cut? I wanted it long, so you could go out in town and operate."

"We were told that you wanted us to cut our hair, sir." We suspected that Delta had tried to disqualify us from the op. General Garrison gave the op to us anyway. "The four of you are going to be the hinge pin of the operation," he said, then filled us in.

We hooked up with Signals Intelligence (SIGINT), run by a CIA communications officer. Their team would gather information by intercepting signals between people (communications intelligence) and electronic signals emitted from enemy technology such as radios, radars, surface-to-air missile systems, aircraft, and ships (electronic intelligence). Most of our SIGINT team spoke two or three languages, and they had aircraft dedicated to their mission.

Next, we met the CIA operations officer, a black Vietnam veteran code-named Condor. Senior to him was the deputy chief of station, an Italian American code-named Leopard. They answered to the thickly built, thick-mustached CIA chief of station, Garrett Jones, code-named Crescent. In Somalia, the CIA agents had their work cut out for them—it's hard to steal a government's secrets where there is no government.

Before our arrival, Washington hadn't allowed the CIA to operate in town, considering it too dangerous. With us on the scene, the spies could penetrate into downtown Mogadishu. The CIA gave us an excellent briefing about Mogadishu, including some culture and history.

Our safe house would be called Pasha, the title of a high-ranking person in the Ottoman Empire. Ahmed would serve as our interpreter. Behind his round-framed glasses, his eyes seldom looked directly at me when he talked—Ahmed always seemed nervous. Our main Somali operative was Mohammed. Constantly risking his life, he was always serious.

After meeting with the CIA we requisitioned four AT-4 missile launchers, tear gas (CS) grenades, flashbangs, and fragmentation grenades. Also, we requested an SST-181 beacon so aircraft flying overhead could get a fix on our area if they needed to. We had to prepare to defend the safe house in case the enemy attacked—and prepare our escape in case they overran us.

That night, we stayed in the hangar with the rest of the American military, about 160 men in all. Each soldier had a 4'×8' place to call his own. Hawks swooped down and caught rats the size of small dogs, flying them back up to the rafters for dinner. Sections of the tin walls had space between them, allowing Mother Nature in. The hangar doors were stuck open. Beyond the doors, helicopters sat quietly on the tarmac, filling the air with the smell of fuel. I could see lights and fires in Mogadishu and taste the salt in the air from the ocean behind our hangar. Aidid sent three mortar rounds near the hangar to wish us good night. Someone wisely turned out the hangar lights.

AUGUST 28, 1993   Saturday, we encrypted our PRC-112 handheld survival radios before gearing up. Outside, the tarmac simmered under our feet as we walked to our helicopter.

Some Delta boys were on board the chopper ready to take off on a training flight.

The Task Force 160 helicopter pilots, among the best in the world, told Delta, "Hey, sorry, we got a real-world op. You know, you need to let these guys on."

The Delta boys were not happy. "Heaven forbid; we wouldn't want to stand in the way of a *real-world op.*"

"Tell you about it when we get back." The Delta operators became smaller and smaller as we gained altitude.

The chopper flew us inland so we could look for routes and alternate routes to drive to and from our safe house. Sunshine and war had blasted much of the color out of Mogadishu. The only structures held sacred by both sides in the civil war had been the Islamic mosques. Many of the other major buildings had been destroyed. People lived in mud huts with tin roofs in a maze of dirt roads. Hills of broken concrete, twisted metal, and trash rose from the landscape, with charred car frames scattered about. Militiamen wielding AK-47s rode in the back of a speeding pickup truck. Fires steadily burned from piles of rubbish, metal drums, and tires. It looked like flames from hell.

Turning back toward the ocean, we scouted out possible landing zones near our safe house—just in case we had to call in a helo to get out in a hurry. During our flyover, we also checked the seashore for possible locations where we could be extracted by boat. Light brown and white sand bordered the emerald sea. It would've been the perfect setting for a vacation resort.

After our reconnaissance, we drove a Humvee from the compound through a secret hole in the back fence to a trailer where the CIA gave us a human intelligence (HUMINT) brief. Technological gizmos and doodads are useful in the spy game, but they mean little without brave human beings to infiltrate the enemy's territory and ask the right questions.

Using a diagram of Pasha, Little Big Man made plans for getting to the safe house and setting up. He delegated the patrol order to me and the course of action for battle stations to Casanova. Little Big Man also worked out the communications drills. Sourpuss loved the training aspect of SEAL Team Six, swimming and running, but when it came to actually operating, he fell behind us in talent and desire. Although he should've played a more central role in leading and planning, he limited his role to setting up who would stand watch on Pasha's roof at what times. The four of us also began constructing a large mosaic map of the city.

"This is your show," Crescent told us. "If your cover is compromised, General Garrison will get you out of there within fifteen minutes. Good luck."

AUGUST 29, 1993   Under the black cloak of Sunday morning, we flew on a Black Hawk helicopter three miles northwest across town to the Mogadiscio Stadium—

Somalia's national stadium for soccer and other events, seating thirty-five thousand people. Because it housed the Pakistani UN troops' compound, we called it the Pakistani Stadium. From there, we loaded onto three indigenous trucks. Only needing two trucks, we used a third as a decoy and backup. It seemed a miracle these trucks even ran. The Somalis used things until they were no longer mechanically viable. Then they used them some more. Someone did a pretty good job of keeping those pieces of crap running.

Mogadishu smelled like urine and human excrement mixed with that tangible smell of starvation, disease, and hopelessness. The odor hung in the air like a dark cloud. It made my heart feel heavy. The Somalis dumped raw sewage in the streets. It didn't help that they used trash and animal dung to fuel the fires that constantly burned in rusted metal barrels. Elementary-school-age boys carried AK-47 rifles. We'd heard that cholera ran rampant because of a nasty water supply. Mogadishu seemed like the end of the world in *I Am Legend*—our mission was to stop the mobs of evil Darkseekers and save the good Somali humans. *No problem, we're SEALs. This is what we do.*

At Pasha, four Somali guards armed with AK-47s opened the iron gates for us. Four others would rotate with them in shifts. Their skinny arms weren't much thicker than the width of three fingers, making the AK-47s appear huge in comparison.

Pasha stood two stories tall and was surrounded by an enormous concrete wall, the house of a wealthy doctor who left with his family when Somalia became too volatile for them. Robbers liked to frequent our area, where the more affluent lived.

I'm sure that when the doctor left, he took all the nice furniture. We had a basic table to sit around at mealtime. I had a cotlike bed made out of 2×4s and a thin mattress. We couldn't drink the water unless we ran it through our Katadyn pump for filtering out dangerous microbes. Sometimes we boiled it. For the most part, we brought in cases of bottled water. But compared to living in a shack and sleeping in the dirt like most people in the city did, we lived like kings.

Even though the guards were obviously undernourished, they wouldn't try to take our leftover food. We had to coax them to take it. Except for the items containing pork, which they wouldn't eat because they were Muslim, we gave them our MREs. They would only eat a small amount themselves and take the rest home for their families. Also, we gave them our empty water bottles, which they used as water storage containers. Often they'd shake our hands and touch their heart as a sign of appreciation and respect. Our interpreter told us that the guards were happy the Americans had arrived. They appreciated that we'd left our families and were risking our lives to help them. Maybe the media wanted to represent America as bullies, but they missed the rest of the story. I think most of the Somalis wanted us to help them end the civil war.

In the big house next to Pasha on the right was the Italian ambassador's residence. Italy had occupied Somalia from 1927 to 1941. In 1949, the UN gave Italy trusteeship of parts of Somalia. Then, in 1960, Somalia became independent. Now the Italians were real bastards, playing both sides of the fence. Whenever the Black Hawks spun up for an operation, the Italians flashed their lights to let the locals know the Americans were coming. Their soldiers employed electric shock on a Somali prisoner's testicles, used the muzzle of a flare gun to rape a woman, and took pictures of their deeds.

The UN accused the Italians of paying bribes to Aidid and demanded that Italy's General Bruno Loi be replaced. The Italian government told the UN to stop harassing Aidid.

One of Italy's main players was Giancarlo Marocchino, who left Italy, following allegations of tax evasion and married a Somali woman in one of Aidid's clans. When the UN confiscated weapons from the militia, the Italian military gave them to Giancarlo, who is suspected to have sold them to Aidid.

Italy dumped trillions of lire into Somalia for "aid." With help from people like Aidid, even before he became an infamous warlord, most of the money went into the pockets of Italy's government officials and their cronies like Marocchino. Marocchino also cultivated a close relationship with news correspondents by wining and dining them during their stay in Mogadishu.

Two houses down from Pasha was a Russian military veteran with some intelligence background, now a mercenary. He would work for either side as long as they paid. He and the Italians seemed to be working together.

Condor briefed us on the actions of the assets, who would visit Pasha every day. For example, if an asset was supposed to come to Pasha from the southeast, but he came from the southwest, we knew he'd been made or was under duress, so we would shoot the person following him. Our asset might do something simple like pause for a second at a corner—then the person behind him would eat a bullet. If he paused twice, both people behind him would eat a bullet. Our procedures were covert enough that an enemy wouldn't know a signal was being given, and although we kept the procedures simple enough for our assets to remember, we spent hours reviewing the procedures with them. A SEAL on the roof always covered each asset's entrance and exit to keep him safe—and to keep impostors out. Usually, when an asset arrived in the dark, he wore an infrared chemlight or a firefly (an infrared strobe light). Some people had noble reasons for helping us, but the most common reason was money.

Four SIGINT guys arrived separately from us, using a different infiltration method and route, then set up shop. Their room looked like the NASA control room for launching a rocket into outer space: monitors, control knobs, switches. They also set up their antennas and other gear on the roof. It looked like CNN headquarters.

When our mosaic map of the city was complete, it covered the entire wall of the biggest room in the house. If an asset told us about a threat, we would stick a pin in the location and plan grid coordinates in case we needed to call in an attack on it.

In a separate brief, an asset came in and gave us possible locations of Mohamed Farrah Aidid, the Somali warlord. We stuck more pins in the map: Olympic Hotel, an officer's barracks, etc. Then we sent the eight-digit coordinates to Crescent, back at the CIA trailer up on the hill.

That same day, back at the base, twenty mortar rounds hit the airfield, tactical operations center, and CIA headquarters. A round hit so close to the CIA trailer that it blew out the windows. Aidid's men had figured out that assets had been going to the trailer. The mortar round had just missed us by a day.

We doubled our watch at Pasha and explained the "grab-and-go" to everyone: grabbing the SIGINT encryption devices, loading them in a rucksack, destroying the other SIGINT gear with a thermite grenade, meeting up at a rendezvous point, then moving out to the extraction area.

That first night, Casanova and I kept watch from the roof. A horrible smell like the remains of a dead carcass filled the air. "What the hell is that?"

AUGUST 30, 1993   On Monday, I looked around the neighborhood for the source of the stench, but it had disappeared. While I fixed tea downstairs, an asset arrived with some information. I brought him some tea.

He politely refused.

"No, it's OK," I said.

He only took half a cup, as though I had given him something of great value. These Somalis conducted themselves so as never to take away too much.

SIGINT told us they'd picked up a conversation between one of Aidid's fire controllers and the mortarmen he was directing. The fire controller advised, "Don't chew your khat until the adjustments and battle damage assessments are made." Khat, a flowering plant native to Somalia, contains a stimulant in the leaves that causes excitement, loss of appetite, and euphoria. A user would chew a wad of leaves as if it were chewing tobacco. Most of Aidid's mortarmen were enticed to do their job for khat. They became dependent on Aidid's people to continue feeding their addiction. Because the drug suppressed appetite, Aidid didn't need to feed them much. They were obviously not well disciplined. Although nothing happened this time, later SIGINT would vector in military strikes and succeed in destroying some of the mortar positions.

That evening, the smell came back. "What the hell *is* that?" I came down off the roof and covertly went next door. On the front porch, I saw a teenaged boy sleeping on a futon. At a distance of around 10 yards, it was obvious I'd found the source of the stench. Later, I found out the fourteen-year-old Somali boy had stepped on a land mine in his school playground. His right foot was blown completely off. Part of his left foot was missing. Gangrene had set in. Aidid's people had planted explosives in the schoolyard to kill or maim children, preventing them from growing up to be effective fighters—turning them into liabilities. The infection in the boy's leg stank so badly that his family couldn't sleep at night with him in the house. So they made him sleep on the porch. During the day, they brought him back inside. I asked the CIA for permission to help the crippled boy next door. They denied my request, not wanting to compromise the safe house.

We noticed a lot of movement between 2200 and 0400 from the street in front of Pasha and surrounding buildings. Based on a tip that Aidid's people hung out there, at 0300, Delta Force fast-roped onto a house. They captured nine people, but they were only UN employees and their Somali guards. Delta had launched on a dry hole.

AUGUST 31, 1993   Aidid was slippery. Rather than stay home, he lived with relatives, staying in the same place only one or two nights. Sometimes he traveled in a motorcade. Sometimes he only used one vehicle. He would dress as a woman. Although he was popular within his own clan, people outside Aidid's clan didn't like him.

Casanova and I dressed up like locals and ran a vehicular route reconnaissance in a Jeep Cherokee that had been beaten more than once with an ugly stick. Secretly, our vehicle was armored. I wore a turban, a flowery Somali shirt, and BDU trousers under my *macawi*. With my beard starting to grow out and dark skin, I could pass for Arab. For weapons we each had a sound-suppressed CAR-15 down between the seats, partly concealed by our skirts. I carried a magazine of ammo in my CAR-15 and an extra in the cargo pocket of my BDU trousers. We also carried our SIG 226 9mms in a breakaway butt pack turned around to the front under our shirts—making it look like we had pooch bellies. To get to my pistol, I could just lift my shirt, reach into the upper right corner, and pull down and away, separating the Velcro and readying my SIG. Besides the magazine of ammo in the pistol, an extra magazine sat in the top of the breakaway butt pack.

Clipped inside my pocket was a Microtech UDT tactical automatic knife, a switchblade—extremely sharp. In the cargo pocket on my right thigh, I carried a blowout kit.

By SEAL standards, we were lightly armed. It was a calculated risk. Traveling light allowed us to blend in better to collect intelligence, but if we were compromised we'd have to run and gun.

We figured out how Aidid's people kept transporting mortar rounds to their crews. I took a picture of two women in colorful robes walking side by side, each carrying a baby in her arms. As I rotated the lens to zoom in, I could clearly see the first baby's head, but the second woman was actually carrying two mortar rounds. The ruse had almost fooled me.

That evening, the boy next door groaned like he was dying. I knew what it was like to be a child in pain. *Screw this*. Casanova, a SIGINT medic named Rick, and I did a hard entry on the boy's house, blacked out with balaclavas and carrying MP-5 machine guns. We didn't take any chances. Kicked in the door. Flexicuffed the boy's mom, dad, and aunt. Put them on the floor next to the wall. Of course, they feared we would kill them. We brought the boy inside, so the parents could see what we were about to do. Rick broke out his supplies. We scrubbed the dead tissue out of the wounds with betadine, a cleaner and disinfectant. It hurt the kid so bad that we had to put our hands over his mouth to keep his screams from waking the neighborhood. He passed out from the pain and shock. We gave him intravenous antibiotics, bandaged his wounds, and injected each butt cheek to stop the infection. Then we vanished.

SEPTEMBER 1, 1993 Wednesday, while conducting observation from the rooftop, we saw an elderly man leading a donkey pulling a wooden cart mounted on an old vehicle axle. On top of the cart were stacks of bricks. During his return trip, he had the same load of bricks. *What?* We asked an asset to follow him. The asset found out the old man hid mortars in the stack of bricks. We reported it. Our superiors issued compromise authority—giving us permission to off the old man.

A sniper must be mentally strong, firmly anchored in a religion or philosophy that allows him to refrain from killing when unnecessary, and to kill when necessary. Shooting can make a person feel powerful, and obviously, a good sniper must not give in to such impulses. On the other hand, through his scope, the sniper becomes intimately familiar with his target, learning his lifestyle and habits, often over a period of time. It's possible to begin to sympathize with the target. The target probably has done nothing to directly hurt the sniper. Yet, when the time comes, the sniper must be able to complete the mission.

On the roof of Pasha, a walkaround wall concealed Casanova and me. I aimed my Win Mag in the old man's direction, 500 yards away.

Casanova viewed him in the spotter scope. "Stand by, stand by. Three, two, one, execute, execute."

Target in my sights, I squeezed the trigger on the first "execute." Right between the eyes—I nailed the donkey.

Expecting to see the old man die, when the donkey dropped instead, Casanova couldn't hold back a little throat chuckle—not very sniperlike.

The old man ran away.

Casanova's throat chuckle sounded like he was gagging.

Later, one of our assets informed us that the old man didn't want to carry the mortars, but Aidid's people threatened to kill his family if he didn't. I felt pretty good about not shooting the old fart.

* * *

The same day, SIGINT guys intercepted communication about a planned mortar attack on the hangar at the army compound. SIGINT knew the mortar crews' communication frequencies. Notifying the base gave the personnel there some time to find cover before seven or eight mortar rounds landed. No friendlies were injured. Just a few minutes' warning is huge.

SIGINT routinely jammed communication between Aidid's fire controllers and the mortarmen. SIGINT vectored in military strikes to destroy the mortar positions. Also, we made khat readily available to the mortar addicts. "You don't need to become Aidid's mortar men to get your fix. Here, go chew this." They smiled like jack-o'-lanterns, their teeth stained black and orange. I know it's a terrible thing to give an addict drugs, but it saved others from being blown to bits by mortar attacks. It probably saved the addicts from dying in one of our military counterstrikes, too. Aidid's people started finding it more difficult to coordinate mortar attacks.

That night, we spotted a man with an AK-47 on the balcony of one of the houses out back and a couple of streets over. I flicked the safety off my sound-suppressed CAR-15 and held the red dot of my sight on his head—an easy shot. Over each of our CAR-15s, we had mounted Advanced Combat Optical Gunsights (ACOGs), a 1.5-power close-range point-and-shoot scope made by Trijicon. At night, it dilated ten times more than my pupil, giving me extra light. Its red dot appears in the scope, unlike a laser that actually appears on the target itself. The ACOG worked just as well in the night as it did in the day. I waited for the man to level his AK-47 in our direction. He never did. After consulting with our guards, we found out the man with the AK-47 was one of our young guards at his own house trying to mimic the SEALs' tactics of defending from the roof. Of course, the idiot never told us of his plans, and he probably couldn't conceive our capability to see him with night vision. We told him, "That was good thinking, but if you're going to be on the rooftop with a weapon at night in this neighborhood, let us know. Because that was almost your ass."

SEPTEMBER 2, 1993   We received the break we needed. Aidid was wealthy, and his college-age daughter had friends in Europe, Libya, Kenya, and other places. Someone slipped her a cell phone, and SIGINT tapped it. Although Aidid moved around a lot, his daughter made a mistake, mentioning on the phone where he was staying. An asset helped pinpoint the house. Our navy spy plane, a P-3 Orion, picked up Aidid's convoy, but the convoy stopped, and we lost him in the maze of buildings. A SIGINT aircraft, having flown in from Europe and now dedicated to us, arrived in the evening to help track and pinpoint Aidid. This tremendously increased our surveillance abilities.

We received a report that Aidid might have acquired portable infrared homing surface-to-air missiles—Stinger missiles—which can be used by someone on the ground to shoot down aircraft.

Casanova, the SIGINT medic, and I did another hard entry on the house of the boy with wounded legs. The family wasn't as scared the second time, but they weren't relaxed, either—a hard entry is a hard entry. We cuffed them again, then held security as we tended to the boy. He looked a lot better and didn't need to scream or pass out as we cleaned him up.

SEPTEMBER 3, 1993   The following morning, we prepared for a trip to the army compound. Our Somali guards did an advance, making a recon of the route before we headed out. During the actual trip, the guards used a decoy that split from us to a different route. Anyone trying to follow would've had to split their forces to follow both vehicles or flip a coin and hope they followed the correct vehicle. Although I received formal training for such tactics, our guards figured this out on their own. Their experiences fighting in the civil war taught them to adapt out of necessity. They were highly intelligent.

The inside of the army compound was fortified with sniper hides, guard towers, and fighting positions. We picked up some infrared chemlights and fireflies in preparation for upgrading Pasha's perimeter security. While there, we also held a meeting with Delta, telling them about the mortar attack details and suspected firing points. They climbed onto the roof of the hangar and did a recon by fire: Snipers shot into suspected areas of mortars and hoped our SIGINT would pick up communication of near hits, verifying locations. When General Garrison found out, he whacked our pee-pees. He didn't like the recon-by-fire action.

Casanova and I hit the house of the wounded teenager again. Mom and Dad obediently took their positions on the floor next to the wall before we put them there. The aunt went down on a knee and held up a tray of tea for us.

I took a drink and offered the family some.

They refused.

We had brought our interpreter with us this time to direct the family as to the boy's care. The family had gone to great lengths to get the tea, and it was all they had. It was the only way they knew to say thank you. They'd been using a witch doctor, but he obviously hadn't been much help in curing the boy.

By now, the stink of the boy's wounds had almost gone. Some of his fever remained. Still, we did another surgical scrub. We gave the family some amoxicillin, an antibiotic for infections. "Give this to the boy three times a day for the next ten days."

I noticed his gums were bleeding. The inside of his mouth was a bloody mess.

"He's got scurvy," our medic said. Vitamin C deficiency.

SEPTEMBER 4, 1993   Casanova and I went out for a drive to recon alternate E&E routes, find out about mortar attack locations, and get a better feel for the area. Later, an asset told us that two mines had been placed on a road and were to be detonated on American vehicles—the same road I'd traveled the day before to meet with Delta at the army compound. They must've found out about our trip and just missed us.

In our neighborhood, little girls walked a mile a day just to get drinking water and carry it back home. A four-year-old washed her two-year-old sister in the front courtyard by pouring water over the top of her. Most Americans don't realize how blessed we are—we need to be more thankful.

By this time, we had become celebrities, controlling a two- to three-block area. When Casanova saw schoolkids, he'd flex and kiss his huge biceps. They imitated him. A small group of kids would gather, and we'd hand out parts of our MREs: candy, chocolate cookies, Tootsie Rolls, and Charms chewing gum. Yes, we gave up our cover, but Condor thought this was good for winning the hearts and minds of the locals. I agreed.

I took a bag of oranges to the crippled boy next door, but he couldn't eat because the citric acid stung his bleeding gums. Casanova held his body down while I put him in a headlock and squirted the liquid into his mouth. After two or three more visits, the oranges didn't sting. Eventually the scurvy would go away. To help the boy, Condor told the CIA that the boy was related to one of our assets even though he wasn't. We had an asset take him some crutches, and I requested a wheelchair.

Later, the boy next door stayed on the porch to spot us when we made our rounds up on the roof of Pasha. He gave us a wave and a smile. It was my most successful op in Somalia, and I had to disobey direct orders to get it done. Better to ask forgiveness than permission.

Aidid ran his own hearts-and-minds campaign. He made public announcements against Americans and started recruiting in our area: anyone from children to the elderly.

Our assets informed us of a trail to be used to supply Aidid with Stinger missiles: Afghanistan to Sudan to Ethiopia to Somalia. The missiles were leftovers from those that the United States gave Afghanistan to fight the Russians. Years later, the United States offered to buy the Stingers back: $100,000 for each one returned with no questions asked.

Aidid received help from al Qaeda and the Palestine Liberation Organization. Al Qaeda had snuck in advisers from Sudan. Not too many people knew about al Qaeda then, but they supplied Aidid with weapons and trained his militia in urban warfare tactics like setting up burning barricades and fighting street to street. If Aidid didn't have the Stingers yet, they'd be arriving soon. In the meantime, al Qaeda taught Aidid's militia to change the detonators on their RPGs from impact detonators to timed detonators. Rather than having to make a direct hit on a helicopter, the RPG could detonate near the tail rotor, the helo's Achilles' heel. Firing an RPG from a rooftop invited death by back blast or the helicopter guns, so al Qaeda taught Aidid's men to dig a deep hole in the street—a militiaman could lie down while the back of the RPG tube blasted harmlessly into the hole. They also camouflaged themselves, so the helos couldn't spot them. Although I didn't know it at the time, the al Qaeda advisers in Somalia probably included Osama Bin Laden's military chief, Mohammed Atef. Similarly, the PLO helped Aidid with advice and supplies. Now Aidid wanted to hit high-profile American targets.

Our SIGINT intercepted communication about a plot to launch a mortar attack on the American Embassy. Furthermore, assets informed us that the Italians continued to allow Aidid's armed militia to cross UN military checkpoints responsible for safeguarding the city. His militia merely had to find out where the Italians had their checkpoints in order to move freely—right into the backyard of the United States and everyone else.

Two of Aidid's bodyguards wanted to give up their master's location for the $25,000 reward. Leopard wanted to meet them at Pasha. To get to Pasha, Leopard planned to travel through the Italian checkpoint near an old pasta factory—Checkpoint Pasta. However, Leopard didn't know that the Italians had secretly turned Checkpoint Pasta over to the Nigerian UN troops. Minutes after the turnover, Aidid's militia ambushed and killed the seven Nigerians.

That evening, I heard a firefight close to Pasha, and the closest mortar yet. Obviously, the bad guys had started to figure out what was going on and where. Our days at Pasha were numbered.

SEPTEMBER 5, 1993   Sunday morning, before 0800, Leopard and four bodyguards rode two Isuzu Troopers out of the UN compound. When the vehicles reached Checkpoint Pasta, a crowd swarmed around them. A couple of hundred yards ahead, burning tires and concrete blocked the road. Leopard's driver floored the accelerator, crashing through the ambush. Forty-nine bullets struck their vehicle. One shot passed through a space in Leopard's flak jacket, striking him in the neck. The driver raced them out of the ambush and helped

Leopard to a hospital in the UN compound. After twenty-five pints of blood and one hundred stitches, General Garrison flew Leopard to a hospital in Germany. Leopard survived.

Later that day, I heard .50 caliber shots, the kind that can penetrate bricks, fired in the northwest 300 to 500 yards from our location.

With shooting nearby and a recent ambush, we knew our ticket was about to get punched. On full alert now, we took up battle stations. That same day, we found out that one of our primary assets had been made, so we had to fly him out of the country.

Then later that evening an asset told us that Aidid was at his aunt's house. Condor called in a helo to fly Stingray and the asset to the army base and brief General Garrison. All of us in Pasha were ecstatic. Everything we had done at Pasha—running the assets, SIGINT, everything—had led to this moment. We had good intel and the cloak of darkness to protect our assault team. The asset even had a diagram for the house—ideal for special operators doing room entries. Aidid was ours.

The request was denied. I still don't know why. Condor and Stingray were outraged. "We will not get another chance this good!"

The rest of us couldn't believe it either. I was angry that we had worked so hard for such an important mission only to be ignored. It seemed that military politics were to blame. I also felt embarrassed at how my own military had treated the CIA. "Condor, I'm really sorry. I don't know what the hell . . . I don't know why we didn't do this . . ."

Condor wasn't mad at us SEALs, but he was mad at General Garrison. "If Garrison isn't going to do it, why did he even send us out here?! Why do all this work, spend all this money, put ourselves at risk, put our assets at risk . . ."

"If we aren't going to pull the trigger," I finished his sentence. "We had Aidid."

"You're damn right we had him!"

At the time, I was mad at Garrison, too. Delta launched on the dry hole at the nearby house, but they couldn't launch when we really had Aidid. It wasn't going to do any good to punch anything or yell at anybody. When I become ultrafurious, I become ultraquiet. After Condor and I shared our misery, I went mute. The others let me have my space. We all mourned the loss of that mission.

SEPTEMBER 6, 1993   In the morning, one of our assets was shot stepping out of his vehicle. Before long, a second asset, our maid's brother, was killed—shot in the head. He was one of the good guys. He wasn't in it for the money as much as he was in it to help his clan end the civil war. She couldn't hide the sadness in her eyes.

As if things weren't bad enough for us, a third asset was beaten almost to death. By the Italians.

A report came in that Aidid possessed antiaircraft guns. Aidid continued to grow stronger and more sophisticated thanks to help from al Qaeda, the PLO, and the Italians turning a blind eye. The locals recognized the growth, too, and were encouraged to join Aidid.

Delta had intelligence that Aidid was in the old Russian compound. So Delta went after him and took seventeen prisoners—but no Aidid. Only two of the seventeen were considered to be of interest. They were detained, interrogated, and then freed. Delta had given Aidid's people another exhibition of how they operate: fly in, fast-rope down, and use a Humvee blocking force of Rangers to protect the operators as they take down the house. This would come back to bite us in the ass.

SEPTEMBER 8, 1993   An asset seemed confident he could get close to Aidid, so we put Delta on alert. As the night grew old, the asset couldn't pinpoint Aidid's position.

Although no communication traffic reached SIGINT, several large explosions came from the direction of the airport. Aidid's mortar crews had figured out how to communicate their fire and control without being intercepted by us. *Damn, they are resilient.*

SEPTEMBER 9, 1993   General Garrison received permission to go to Phase Three—going after Aidid's lieutenants. Delta flew over Mogadishu as a show of force with the entire package: ten to twelve Little Birds and twenty to thirty Black Hawks. Delta snipers rode in the light Little Bird helicopters, which could carry guns, rockets, and missiles. In the medium-sized Black Hawk helicopters, also armed with guns, rockets, and missiles, the Delta entry teams and Rangers had fast ropes ready in the doorway to make an assault at any moment. The idea was to show Aidid our strength—making him less attractive to the local population and, hopefully, hurting his ability to recruit.

On the same day, near the pasta factory, two kilometers away from the Pakistani Stadium, the Army's 362nd Engineers worked to clear a Mogadishu roadway. A Pakistani armored platoon protected them while the Quick Reaction Force (QRF) stood by in case they needed emergency reinforcements. The QRF was made up of men from the conventional army's 10th Mountain Division,

101st Aviation Regiment, and 25th Aviation Regiment, their base located at the abandoned university and old American Embassy.

The engineers bulldozed an obstacle from the road when a crowd of Somalis gathered. One Somali fired a shot, then sped away in a white truck. The engineers cleared a second obstacle. Then the third: burning tires, scrap metal, and a trailer. Someone on a second-story balcony fired at them. Engineers and Pakistanis returned fire. The enemy fire increased, coming at them from multiple directions. The crowd moved obstacles to block the soldiers in. The engineers called in the QRF helos. In three minutes, armed OH-58 Kiowa and AH-1 Cobra helicopters arrived. Hundreds of armed Somalis moved in from the north and south. Enemy RPGs came in from multiple directions.

The Cobra opened up on the enemy with 20 mm cannons and 2.75-inch rockets. More QRF helos were called in for help while the engineers tried to escape, heading for the Pakistani Stadium. Aidid's militia fired a 106 mm recoilless rifle, blasting the lead Pakistani tank into flames. A bulldozer stopped dead, so the engineers abandoned it. As thirty Somalis tried to take the abandoned bulldozer, two TOW missiles destroyed them and the bulldozer. The engineers, two wounded, and the Pakistanis, three wounded, fought on until they reached the stadium. One Pakistani died. It had been the largest battle in Somalia to that point.

Our intelligence sources told us that Aidid had commanded the ambush from the nearby cigarette factory. More than one hundred Somalis died, and hundreds more were wounded, but Aidid had succeeded in keeping the road closed, restricting the UN forces' movement. In addition, the media assisted Aidid by reporting the many "innocent" Somali deaths. *I hate our liberal media.*

Must be easy to sit back and point fingers when you're not involved. President Clinton also helped Aidid, halting combat operations in Mogadishu until an investigation could be completed. *Political popularity trumps American lives.*

Aidid launched artillery over Pasha. Machine-gun fire and fire-fights reached closer to us. We remained on full alert and high pucker factor. Aidid's militia also launched mortars on the Nigerian checkpoint at the Port of Mogadishu—turned over by the Italians.

Condor's assets infiltrated a rally held in a vehicle repair garage where Aidid tried to pump up his troops. If Aidid was actually there at the rally, we wanted to know. He wasn't.

SEPTEMBER 10, 1993   At 0500 the next day, Aidid's militia fired more artillery at the Port of Mogadishu checkpoint. That same day, an asset told us that Aidid's people knew about Pasha. They described our guns and vehicles, and they knew Condor from before we set up Pasha.

Aidid ambushed CNN's Somali crew. Their interpreter and four guards were killed. Aidid's militia had mistaken the CNN's crew for us.

We also found out that an Italian journalist had arranged to do an interview with Aidid. One of our assets put a beacon on the journalist's car, so we could track him. The journalist must've suspected something was wrong, because he went to the house of one of the good guys instead, probably hoping we'd launch an attack there. Fortunately, we had an asset on the ground verifying the location.

Even so, the CIA was screwed. So were we. We had good intel that Aidid's people were going to ambush us. Instead of two SEALs on watch and two resting, we went to three SEALs on watch and one resting.

SEPTEMBER 11, 1993   I finally got to bed at 0700 the next morning—no ambush. Sourpuss woke me up at 1100 to tell me that our assets were reporting that Aidid's militia was closing in on us.

Another asset told us that the bad guys had targeted our head guard, Abdi, because they knew he was working for the CIA. One of the guards in his employ was his own son. The head guard took responsibility for paying the guards; moreover, he had responsibility for their lives. He held an important status in his clan. The head guard put his family and clan at risk to help the CIA. Part of his motivation was money, but the greater motivation seemed to be a better future for his family. Now he was made. Later we would find out who ratted him out: the Italians.

Condor called General Garrison. "We've been compromised, and we need to get the out of here."

At 1500, leaving nonessential equipment such as MREs, everyone in Pasha packed up, and we drove to the Pakistani Stadium. Helicopters extracted us at 1935, taking us back to the hangar on the military compound.

In retrospect, on the first day at Pasha, we should've flexicuffed the Italians and taken them out of the area, and we should've assassinated the Russian mercenary. Then we would've had a better chance of running our safe house and capturing Aidid. Of course, it would've helped if our own military had let us capture Aidid when we had him at his aunt's house.

Although we had lost Pasha, we still had targets to act on.

10.
Capturing Aidid's Evil Genius

SEPTEMBER 12, 1993   Casanova and I walked into the hangar. Several Rangers approached us. "Wish you guys would've been with us when we were ambushed."

We lived with Delta Force, the Combat Control Team (CCT), and pararescuemen (PJs). CCTs were the air force's special operations pathfinders who could parachute into an area and provide reconnaissance, air traffic control, fire support, and command, control, and communications on the ground—particularly helpful to us in calling down death from above. SIGINT drafted many of their people from the CCTs. The air force's PJs, also special operations, focused on rescuing pilots downed in enemy territory and administering medical treatment. Both Delta and SEAL Team Six had begun augmenting their forces with CCTs and PJs. On a SEAL Team Six boat crew of eight men assaulting a building, the addition of a PJ, who could take care of patching up bullet wounds, freed up a SEAL hospital corpsman to kick more doors. Likewise, the addition of a CCT carrying a radio on his back and calling for air support freed up a SEAL radioman to carry other mission-essential gear on his back and help with the door-kicking. Although the air force CCTs and PJs were not as specialized in skills like door-kicking, they were experts in their fields—to a higher level than SEAL or Delta operators. Integrating them into SEAL Team Six and Delta was one of the best moves JSOC ever made.

One of our CCTs was Jeff, a pretty boy who was a woman magnet like Casanova; they even hung around together sometimes. Another CCT was Dan Schilling, a thirty-year-old laid-back Southern Californian. Dan left the Army Reserves to become a CCT. Tim Wilkinson quit his electrical engineering job for the adventure of becoming a PJ. Scotty served as the PJs' team leader.

At 2100, we received mortar fire, now becoming such a regular occurrence that guys in the hangar cheered. Some had a mortar pool going. A person could buy a time slot for a dollar. Whoever chose a slot closest to the actual time the mortar hit won the pool.

No one had leads on Aidid.

SEPTEMBER 13, 1993   A Pakistani convoy came in to resupply. Under General Garrison's orders, Casanova and I rode with Steve (a Delta sniper working a lot with military intelligence), Commander Assad, and Assad's Pakistani troops. We drove across town to the northwest, near Pakistani Stadium, where the Pakistanis ran a tight compound. Their troops exhibited excellent military bearing and a by-the-book attitude. They kept the area tidy. Nothing like the sloppy Italians who were constantly trying to undermine us.

During the night, Aidid's militia fired on one of our helicopters, using the abandoned Somali National University as their sniper hide. Casanova and I climbed six stories to the top of a tower. From there, we could see the house of Osman Ali Atto—Aidid's financier and evil genius. Atto allegedly used income from drug trafficking (mostly khat), arms trafficking, looting, and kidnapping to buy more weapons and support for Aidid's militia. Next to Atto's house stood his vehicle repair garage, an enormous open-top concrete building where his mechanics worked on cars, bulldozers, and technicals—pickup trucks with .50 caliber machine guns on tripods bolted onto the truck bed. This was the same garage where Aidid had held the rally to pump up his militia while we were in Pasha. *If we capture Atto, we cut off the financial support for Aidid's militia. He who controls the purse strings controls the war.*

SEPTEMBER 14, 1993   We continued to observe Atto's garage. People constantly came and went. Three mechanics worked on vehicles. Casanova and I spotted someone who looked like Atto, flashing a big white smile, having a meeting.

We took a picture, then transmitted the data by a secure link back to the intel guys so they could make sure the man in the garage really was Atto. We lost him when he left the garage and drove away.

The same day, a Ranger thought he spotted Aidid in a convoy. Delta hit a building to find out they had captured General Ahmed Jilao instead, even though Jilao was much taller, heavier, and lighter-skinned than Aidid—and was a close ally of the United Nations. Aidid had become like Elvis—people saw him where he wasn't.

At night, the Pakistani compound received fire from the area of nearby trees and buildings. Commander Assad said, "We keep receiving fire from there on a regular basis. Can you help us?"

"We can spot them with our infrared scopes and fire tracers at them, and your machine gunners can open fire on that area." (The tracers are phosphorous covered rounds that burn with a glow.)

Allah was with those militiamen—they didn't fire again that evening.

SEPTEMBER 16, 1993   We told a Delta captain, "We'd like to do night sniper flights with the QRF: eyes over Mogadishu."

"OK."

The first time Casanova and I rode in a QRF helo, we found out their rules of engagement allowed them to keep a magazine in their weapon but no round in the chamber until an enemy fired at them. We always kept a round in our chamber, so all we had to do was flick off the safety switch and shoot. In a war zone, the QRF's rules of engagement were ludicrous.

One day, Casanova and I boarded a Humvee with the QRF. I said, "Lock and load."

The soldiers gave me a strange look. "What the?" Gradually, the lightbulbs came on. Each man made sure his weapon was still on safe and loaded a round in the chamber. Casanova and I would take responsibility for any repercussions from the army brass.

The next time some Rangers, Casanova, and I drove up in our Humvees at the QRF compound, the QRF soldiers who had ridden with Casanova and me before hurried to ride with us again because they knew what our first command would be. "Lock and load."

Later, as more soldiers had an opportunity to ride with us, they'd be standing in line waiting to see which of the Humvees Casanova and I drove up in. We laughed at the sight of them fighting to see who would ride in our vehicle.

SEPTEMBER 17, 1993 We found out that Atto would have a meeting in his garage the next day at 0730. Our human intelligence was amazing, telling us exactly when and where a meeting would be taking place for Atto. Unfortunately, we couldn't acquire that kind of intel for Aidid as we had before. Delta launched on the radio station to capture Aidid but hit another dry hole.

That evening, Casanova stayed in the tower while I snuck over to the edge of the Pakistani compound and looked over the wall at the adjacent Save the Children house. There was just too much activity going on in the dark of early morning and night. Later, HUMINT sources told us that one of the Somali drivers secretly used the trunks of the cars to transport weapons and ammunition, including mortar rounds. Flying the Save the Children flag on their vehicle, they could drive through almost any roadblock unchecked. I don't think that the people at the Save the Children compound knew the drivers were using their vehicles in this way, but it answered a lot of questions for us about equipment and ammo transportation.

SEPTEMBER 18, 1993 Casanova and I began surveillance on Atto's garage from the Pakistani tower at 0600.

A CIA asset had to go inside the garage and verify that the person was indeed Atto before we launched the full package—at least a hundred men, including a Humvee blocking force, Little Birds with Delta snipers, and Black Hawks with Rangers and Delta operators. To signal us, our asset would walk to the middle of the garage area, remove his red and yellow cap with his right hand, and walk around. Casanova and I would then call in the full package—an enormous responsibility for two enlisted men.

At 0745 the CIA asset, mustache on his long face, wearing a red and yellow cap, a blue T-shirt, and a *macawi* made out of blue and white plaid material, appeared at the garage. He would earn $5,000 if he succeeded in fingering Atto. After twenty-five minutes he still hadn't given the predetermined signal. Then Atto arrived, sporting his Cheshire cat grin. His bodyguards and an old man arrived with him. We radioed it in, but we were required to have the asset's confirmation before launching the package.

Instead of giving us the signal nonchalantly, the asset acted like he'd seen too many B-movies or we were stupid. He took his hand straight out to the side, reached in an arc to the top of his hat, pulled his hat straight up, reversed the arc, and lowered it to his side. If I'd been one of Atto's guards, I would've shot the idiot in the head right then. I fully expected him to be executed before our eyes, but no one had noticed his exaggerated act.

Casanova and I launched the full package. The QRF went on standby. Little Birds and Black Hawks filled the sky. Soon Delta Force operators fast-roped down inside the garage, Rangers fast-roped around the garage, and Little Birds flew around with snipers giving the assault force protection. Atto's people scattered like rats. Militia appeared in the neighborhood, shooting up at the helicopters. News reporters showed up, and sniper Dan Busch threw flashbangs to scare them away from walking into a kill zone. It would later be erroneously reported that hand grenades were thrown at the crew. *Ungrateful idiots. A hand grenade thrown at that range would've killed them all.* Dan personally told me later that the Bat Phone rang from the Pentagon, and he had to explain to the higher-ups that he wasn't throwing fragmentation grenades.

Having crawled over the ledge of a retaining wall and out to the lip of our six-story tower, I lay prone—four rounds loaded in my Win Mag with a fifth in the chamber. Casanova covered the left half of Atto's garage area. I took the right. Through my Leupold 10-power scope, I saw a militiaman 500 yards away firing through an open window at the helos. I shot him in the chest. He fell backward into the building, instantly dead.

Another militiaman carrying an AK-47 came out a fire escape

and at the Delta operators assaulting. From 300 yards my shot passed through him. He dropped on the spot.

Then I saw a guy about 800 yards away aimed an RPG launcher at the helicopters.

He was well out of the range of what General Garrison had made all of us focus on: the shots we could hit every time. I'd never made a killing shot in combat at this distance.

There was no time to dial in my scope properly. I had to go half on instinct and experience. I dialed in at 1,000 yards—I could mentally calculate the distances under that—but in my rush to beat Mr. RPG to the trigger, I forgot to properly adjust the mil dots. My estimate was rougher than I knew.

Putting the crosshairs on Mr. RPG's upper sternum, I squeezed the trigger on the most important shot of my life. And missed the bull's-eye.

Because of the miscalculation, the bullet didn't hit him in the heart as I'd planned.

It hit him square in the head, right underneath his nose.

People picture that when a guy gets shot, he flies backward, but the opposite is often true. The bullet penetrates at such a high velocity that it actually pulls the man forward as it goes through, causing him to fall on his face. This militiaman pulled the trigger of the RPG as he fell forward, firing it straight down into the street below. *Boom!*

Hovering overhead in the Little Birds, Delta snipers saw me make the shot. Minutes later, one of the choppers buzzed our tower. "Hell, yeah!" the snipers yelled, giving me the thumbs-up. I was glad Casanova and I had been lying prone, because the windblast of the snipers' chopper came close to blowing us off our six-story tower.

Delta took fifteen prisoners, but the Rangers in the Humvees hadn't arrived in time to secure the area by cordoning off vehicle and foot traffic. Atto had exchanged shirts with one of his lieutenants and walked out the back of his garage—slipping away.

SEPTEMBER 19, 1993   In the dark hours of morning, I woke up to the QRF pulling a raid on houses 500 yards north of our position. The QRF took small-arms fire and RPGs. Aidid's militia chose the wrong convoy to fire on that morning. From the tower, with my night vision, I had an excellent view of the enemy. I picked up the radio mike and vectored helo fire to the source of Aidid's militia. The QRF helo showered down .50 caliber and 40 mm rounds, and QRF ground forces assaulted so heavily that the sky vibrated and the earth shook. The few enemy who survived couldn't get out of there fast enough, running for their lives past Casanova's and my position.

We had used the tower effectively, but Aidid's people put two and two together. A Somali woman stopped and looked up at us. Then she gave Casanova and me the throat-cutting sign. We decided our sniper hide in the Pakistani tower had been compromised and received permission to close it for a few days.

We left the Pakistani compound at 1700 and arrived in the hangar at around 1730. Half a dozen Delta snipers met us at the front door, high-fiving me. "Wasdin, you rock!" One of them looked at the other Delta snipers. "If I ever have someone shooting at me, I want Wasdin making those thousand-yard headshots!"

Later, Casanova and I lasered the actual distance of the head shot: 846 yards, making it the longest killing shot of my career. It also improved our relations with Delta. I never told them I was aiming for the guy's chest.

SEPTEMBER 20, 1993   At 0230, Casanova and I took a QRF flight until 0545. During the flight, we spotted a man erecting a mobile transmitter. We thought we'd found the location of Aidid's Radio Mogadishu, where he transmitted operation orders, how to fire mortars, and propaganda. *The UN and Americans want to take over Somalia, burn the Koran, and take your firstborn children.* Even when Aidid's militia got its butt kicked, Radio Mogadishu broadcasted cries of victory, keeping his own people motivated and encouraging other Somalis to join his winning team. Casanova and I couldn't shoot a man for raising a transmitter, but we marked the location as the possible location of Aidid's station.

The QRF aircrew asked if we could fly with them all week. They'd been shot at enough that they wanted SEAL snipers.

Later that day at the compound, Condor contacted us. One of his assets reported that Atto would be at his house for a meeting. The four of us were the only operators who had frequently seen Atto and could ID him. Condor wanted a SEAL to go along with him and some Delta operators. We selected Casanova, but the mission was scrubbed. Our QRF flight got canceled, too. Although we'd loaded up the Humvees for an assault on Atto's house, that was also canceled. *Jock up, stand down, jock up—and every time might be the last.* The stand-downs bothered me, but not to the point of weakening my motivation to jock up again. Whatever the challenges, I knew I had to pick myself up and keep trying. I grew up with a knot in the pit of my stomach, a perpetual state of worry over when my father would come after me. At

BUD/S, Instructor Stoneclam told us, "I can make anybody tough, but it takes someone special for me to make mentally tough." Although SEALs are known for their small numbers and efficiency, the military as a whole is huge and cumbersome—requiring us to be patient. My Teammates and I shared a similar mindset. We had learned how to control feelings of frustration. I knew I could overcome the challenges of a fluid environment. Nothing ever goes exactly as planned. Even with the best plan, when the bullets start flying, that plan is going to change.

SEPTEMBER 21, 1993   Our asset Abe reported sighting Osman Atto in Lido near our old safe house, Pasha. In dealing with human intel, we always had to figure out what was real and what was made up for personal gain. I don't think any of our assets out-and-out lied to us, but they would exaggerate, probably to get more money. Abe didn't seem to be doing this just for the money. Soft-spoken, he wouldn't become anxious like the others. He talked calmly and matter-of-factly. We liked working with "honest Abe."

In the movie *Black Hawk Down,* someone marks the roof of Atto's vehicle with what looks like olive green military rubber-based adhesive duct tape (riggers' tape). That would've stuck out like a turd in a punch bowl. What really happened was like something out of a James Bond movie. The CIA's Office of Technical Services in Langley mounted a homing beacon inside an ivory-handled cane as a gift for Aidid, but the mission was scrubbed. Condor resurrected the cane and gave it to Abe, who passed it to a contact who met regularly with Atto. The contact would give it to Atto as a gift. While the contact with the cane rode in a car to northern Mogadishu, a helicopter in the air followed the beacon.

TOP: Ben Wilbanks and Howard as a child.

MIDDLE: *(Back row, left to right)* Howard with his sisters, Sue Ann and Tammy. *(Front row, left to right)* Howard's stepfather, Leon, and mother, Millie.

BOTTOM: Howard, fighting in a Navy Smokers boxing match (his back is to the camera).

US Navy Aircrew, Search and Rescue Team. HS-1 Jax. Flo.

Howard   Bobby   Kriv   Mock

TOP: Jacksonville, Florida HS-1 Aircrew Search and Rescue Team: Howard, Bobby, Kriv, and Mark.

BOTTOM: Howard, reenlisting to attend BUD/S training.

TOP LEFT: SAR training. *(Courtesy U.S. Navy)*

TOP RIGHT: "Drownproofing" in BUD/S. *(Courtesy U.S. Navy)*

BOTTOM: Howard, graduating from BUD/S.

TOP: Howard at winter warfare training in Alaska.

BOTTOM LEFT: Howard inside a tent during winter warfare training.

BOTTOM RIGHT: More winter warfare training.

TOP: Aiming an MP-5N while maintaining security on the upper deck of a ship for training. *(Courtesy U.S. Navy)*

BOTTOM: Inside an H-3 helicopter before an actual assault on an enemy ship.

TOP: A SEAL fast-roping onto a ship. *(Courtesy U.S. Navy)*

BOTTOM: Air Force jets fly over burning Kuwaiti oil rigs during Operation Desert Storm. *(Courtesy U.S. Air Force)*

TOP: Howard, reenlisting during sniper training.

BOTTOM LEFT: Howard's ghillie suit during sniper training at Quantico, Virginia.

BOTTOM RIGHT: Sniper class patch.

<small>TOP:</small> A sniper in his ghillie suit. *(Courtesy Department of Defense)*

<small>MIDDLE:</small> Casanova preparing for a training dive.

<small>BOTTOM:</small> Inside Pasha, SIGINT room.

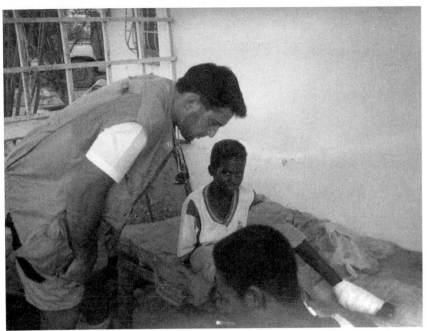

TOP: Helping a child with an amputated leg.

BOTTOM: Pasha team: *(kneeling in front, left to right)* Little Big Man, Casanova, Howard, and Sourpuss.

TOP: Howard, on the roof of Pasha, wielding an AT-4.

BOTTOM: The view from a Pakistani tower—Otto Osman's house and garage are in the distance. *(Osman's house circled in white)*

TOP: The woman on the left carries a baby, while the woman on the right pretends to carry a baby but is really carrying mortar rounds to supply Aidid.

MIDDLE: SEAL Humvee. *(Courtesy U.S. Navy)*

BOTTOM: Confiscated enemy small arms and crew weapons. *(Courtesy Department of Defense)*

TOP: K-4 Circle where Little Big Man was shot. *(Courtesy Department of Defense)*

BOTTOM: U.S. peacekeepers under attack in Somalia. *(Courtesy Department of Defense)*

TOP: SEAL Team Six and Delta operators.

BOTTOM: Michael Durant, the downed Black Hawk pilot, and Howard.

TOP: Silver Star ceremony: *(back row, left to right)* unknown, Sourpuss, Howard, and Homer. *(Front row, left to right)* Little Big Man, unknown, unknown, and Eric Olson.

ABOVE LEFT: Howard's Silver Star.

ABOVE RIGHT: Howard's Purple Heart.

RIGHT: Ambassador Negroponte. *(Courtesy State Department)*

TOP: Thanksgiving at U.S. Ambassador Negroponte's residence in the Philippines. Howard is on the right, and the Ambassador was taking the picture.

BOTTOM: Training the security contingent for the 1996 U.S. Olympics in Atlanta.

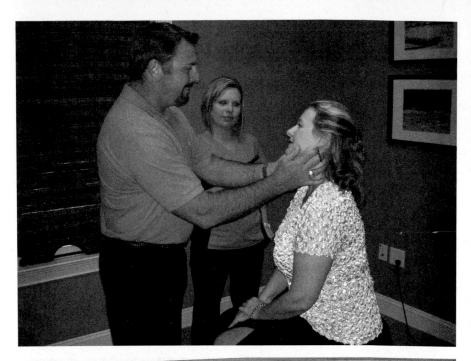

TOP: Howard in his clinic adjusting a patient.

BOTTOM: Howard's wife, Debbie, with Howard and their children, Blake and Eryn.

When the car stopped for gas, Atto materialized. An asset called Condor to let him know that Atto was in the car. Condor radioed Delta.

Delta launched. The assault helo landed almost on top of the target vehicle, and a sniper fired into the engine block, stopping it—the first helicopter takedown on a moving vehicle. Atto threw open the car door and fled. The bodyguard fired his AK-47 at the assault team, but a sniper shot the bodyguard in the leg, disabling him. Assaulters jumped out of the helo, rushed the building, and captured Atto.

Other Delta guys formed a perimeter around the building. The Somalis burned tires to signal others for help. A few probed Delta's perimeter. A crowd formed. AK-47 and RPG rounds were shot at the helos. Delta snipers in one helo and the guns on another helo fired at the enemy, taking ten to twenty of them down, and pushing back the mob.

Inside, Delta took Atto to the top of the building, where a helo landed and picked them up.

Later, back at the compound, Delta asked us, "We're not sure if it's Atto or not. Could you guys come over and verify his identification?"

"Hell, yeah." Casanova and I walked over to the other end of the runway near the CIA building where they were holding Atto captive in a CONEX box. In *Black Hawk Down,* he was a large man who wore nice clothes, coolly smoked a cigar, and ridiculed his captors. In reality, although he dressed in semiformal shirt and *macawi,* he sniveled. Short, skinny as a broom handle, and shaking like a leaf, Atto looked at Casanova and me like we were the Grim Reaper coming to dispose of him. I almost felt sorry for Atto. Part of me wanted to give him a hug and say, "It'll be OK," and part of me wanted to shoot him in the face.

"Yeah, this is him," Casanova said.

"I don't know," I joked. "Every time we saw him before, he was smiling a big white smile."

Casanova looked at the interpreter. "Tell him if he doesn't smile we're going to beat the crap out of him."

Before the interpreter could translate, Atto flashed a fake smile.

We hadn't realized Atto spoke English. Casanova and I high-fived each other. "That's him!"

Delta whisked him away to a prison on an island off the coast of Somalia. A note found on Atto advised him to meet with reporters to set up a negotiation session with the United Nations Operation in Somalia (UNOSOM). We assume the note was from Aidid—the big fish we still wanted to catch.

11.
Eyes over Mogadishu Mission

To capture Aidid, we'd have to overcome the military game of Red Light, Green Light. We'd be told that there wasn't good intel to act on. Suddenly, we'd get the green light to act on something. Then someone above would cancel our mission before we lifted off the ground.

SEPTEMBER 22, 1993   While we sat on our cots in the hangar, the JSOC sergeant major came over and shot the bull with us. He wisely recommended that we mingle more with Delta operators, particularly the assaulters from Charlie Squadron. In some ways SEALs were quite similar to Delta. For instance, we both excelled at door-banging and shooting. In other ways, though, we were quite different—for instance, takedowns of ships vs. planes. The busy tempo of ops, often done separately, added to the difficulty of getting together with Delta. Plus, in the highly competitive environment of special operations units, especially at the tier-one level, some Delta operators seemed jealous of us. We were tightest with the Delta snipers because we had the most in common with them, and we hung out with the Air Force CCTs and PJs that we knew from before.

The upper echelon canceled our rides on the QRF flights "to work out kinks." I can only guess that the conventional army leaders of the QRF couldn't get along with the unconventional leaders of Delta.

SEPTEMBER 25, 1993   Even though we and the QRF pilots liked our Eyes over Mogadishu Mission, the upper echelon canceled our evening QRF flights, again. Military politics bounced this back and forth—some nights we were allowed to participate and some nights we weren't—probably because someone above didn't like sharing his piece of pie with Delta and the SEALs.

That night, Aidid's militia used an RPG to shoot down one of the QRF helicopters. The pilot and copilot were injured, and three others died. Aidid supporters had mutilated the dead soldiers' bodies while the pilot and copilot evaded capture. The Pakistanis and United Arab Emirates (UAE) forces secured the area within minutes, protecting the surviving pilot and copilot as well. Our PJs, with us in support, were ready to rescue the survivors within fifteen minutes, but it was the opinion of all of us in the hangar that the QRF leadership was too ineffectual to do their job properly and too proud to let us help. It took QRF's Search and Rescue two hours to arrive. Totally unacceptable. Not only did the QRF leave their pilot and copilot vulnerable, they also endangered the Pakistanis and UAE forces protecting them on the ground. Where was the *quick* in the Quick Reaction Force? *If Casanova and I had been on that flight, we probably could've saved them.*

Some in the military thought that this RPG shooting down a Black Hawk was a fluke. The RPG was made for ground-to-ground fighting, not ground-to-air. Aiming one at the air meant the back blast would bounce off the street and probably kill the shooter. Also, the white rocket trail marked the shooter's position for helicopter gunfire to take him out. The Black Hawk seemed too fast and too well armored to be shot down by such a weapon. The military would be proved wrong.

SEPTEMBER 26, 1993   In the evening, a .50 caliber antiaircraft weapon was being set up at the pasta factory, and the next day it was dismantled and hidden. Aidid's people had seen how we operated on more than one occasion. Now they were preparing to shoot us out of the sky. They were smarter than we gave them credit for.

SEPTEMBER 27, 1993   We got a location on Colonel Abdi Hassan Awale (a.k.a. Abdi Qeybdid), Aidid's interior minister. We jocked up with the helo and ground forces, but we had to cancel the mission because Aidid was supposedly sighted elsewhere, and they wanted us to stand by to chase Elvis.

The CIA, SIGINT, and military counterintelligence took eleven guys into custody who were believed to be the controllers and launchers of the enemy mortar teams.

SEPTEMBER 28, 1993   We went to the memorial service in the 10th Mountain Division hangar for the three men who died in the QRF helo crash. Condor attended. After the service, he told me, "We've got a lot of targets, but all the military red tape and smoke prevents us from touching them." He was clearly disgusted.

The QRF had difficulties working with Delta. Delta had difficulties working with the CIA. Beyond those difficulties were the problems within the United Nations, particularly Italy. The Clinton administration's lack of support compounded the mess. The three QRF bodies were loaded onto the plane to fly home.

Later that day, although I didn't want to, we got together with Delta on the runway for a group picture. I unhappily stood at the back of the group. *Why are we doing this? So someone can get a copy and target each of us individually?* I was told to do it, so I did. Looking back, I'm glad. It's the only picture I have of my buddy Dan Busch, a sniper in Delta Force's Charlie Squadron, standing next to me. It's my only picture of others, too. Sometimes I look at this picture, which I keep in my personal office, and honor their memory.

SEPTEMBER 30, 1993   Around noon, we received a report that Qeybdid had been sighted. We prepared to go, but the reconnaissance bird lost him, and we didn't launch. Finding one man in the maze of Mogadishu was like finding a mole inside an elephant's butt. We should've taken him when we had the chance before, but instead, we chased Elvis sightings.

OCTOBER 2, 1993   In the afternoon, we geared up to hit Aidid at Sheik Aden Adere's house. We stood on alert for three and a half hours. Aidid had been at the same house for four hours. Again, the CIA seemed to have a sure thing, but the hit didn't go down. The Agency was furious.

OCTOBER 3, 1993   When I woke up, the CIA told me they wanted to set up a couple of radio repeaters in the Lido district of Mogadishu. An asset could use his handheld radio to transmit to the repeater, which could relay the transmission back to the army compound. Likewise, the base could transmit to the asset using the repeater. This would allow for stronger radio transmission at longer distances.

I wore desert cammies with body armor underneath, including the hard armor inserts. Over my cammy top, I put on a bandolier with ten magazines, thirty rounds in each, for a total of three hundred rounds. We rode Huey helicopters out to the Pakistani Stadium, then rode local vehicles to two houses. After inserting the repeaters, we drove to the pick-up point and got onto the helos. I had no idea this was about to be the longest day of my life—and nearly my last.

PART THREE

Do the right thing even if it means dying like a dog when no one's there to see you do it.

—Vice Admiral James Stockdale,
U.S. NAVY PILOT

12.
Battle of Mogadishu

As we pulled back into the compound, everyone was jocking up for something big. Helicopters spun up, Humvees pulled into position, and everyone topped off their magazines.

Commander Olson approached us before we stepped out of our "cutvee"—a cut Humvee without a top, doors, or windows, officially called the M-998 cargo/troop carrier. It had no special armor. Tech reps from the States had arrived less than a week earlier and put a Kevlar ballistic blanket underneath the vehicle to protect against land mines or other fragmentation. I sat in the driver's seat with Casanova riding shotgun. Behind me was Little Big Man, Sourpuss beside him. To the rear of them we had two benches running parallel to the vehicle where two army guys sat—I think they were Rangers, but they could've been Delta operators. In addition, a Ranger manned the .50 caliber machine gun.

Commander Olson briefed us in just a few minutes. Our target was one of Aidid's militia headquarters. "You'll be part of a blocking force. Delta will rope in and assault the building. You guys will grab the prisoners. Then get out of there." Usually a brief would last an hour to an hour and a half. The mission had popped up when we were setting up the repeaters. Commander Olson slapped me on the shoulder. "Shouldn't take long. Good luck. See you when you get back."

Four light AH-6J Little Birds carried four snipers each. The Little Birds also carried rockets underneath—where we would be going wasn't going to be good. Two of the helos would guard the front of the target building from the air while two hovered to the rear. Delta's C Squadron would fast-rope from two more to assault the building. Eight Black Hawks would follow. Two carried Delta assaulters and their ground command. Four would insert the Rangers. One would hover above with a Combat Search and Rescue team. The eighth Black Hawk contained the two mission commanders. One commander would direct the pilots, the other would direct the men on the ground.

Three OH-58D Kiowa helos, distinctive for the black ball mounted above the rotor, would also fly in the airspace above the target. The black ball was a sight with a platform that contained a TeleVision System, a Thermal Imaging System, and a Laser Range Finder/Designator to provide audio and video of the ground to General Garrison at the Joint Operations Center. High above everyone circled a P-3 Orion.

I drove into position at about the third vehicle in the convoy. Behind our Humvees idled three 5-ton trucks, and five more Humvees brought up the rear. Rangers made up most of our convoy. In all, nineteen aircraft, twelve vehicles, and 160 men.

Aidid's men had already seen how we did this six times before, and now we'd be operating under broad daylight on his home turf. Many of his militia would be pumped up on khat at this time of day, not coming down off their high until late in the evening. Risks that pay off are bold moves. Those that don't pay off are stupid. Part of my job included taking risks.

At 1532, the helicopters took off first, following the coast. When we received word that the birds were headed inland, our convoy headed out. I wasn't afraid—yet. *This is going to be a routine op.*

On the way, the lead Humvee took a wrong turn. Nobody

followed. They would have to catch up to us later. We sped forward, meeting sporadic fire. Little Big Man yelled, "Aw hell, I'm hit!"

I pulled off the road underneath an overhang, slammed on the brakes, jumped out, and checked Little Big Man. He lay on the floor with part of his Randall knife blade beside him. I expected to see blood come from somewhere but only found a huge raspberry on his leg. An AK-47 round had hit that Randall knife he loved so much and carried everywhere. The blade lay on the floor. It saved his leg—worth all the kidding he had ever endured about that big-ass knife.

The convoy continued moving during the minute we were parked on the side of the road. I returned to the driver's seat, then sped forward, catching up to our former position.

I didn't know that a mile west of the target, militia gathered at the Bakara Market, distributing smuggled weapons and ammo. To the east, a mile away, was where foreign insurgents had recently arrived. We were already being sandwiched.

In a sandstorm kicked up by the helos, Delta operators roped down to the target building. Delta stacked up near the door, lining up behind each other in preparation to enter and snatch their target. Four groups of Rangers, twelve in each, fast-roped down and sealed the four corners of the city block around the target building. They made up the blocking force. No one gets in, and no one gets out.

I left the cutvee and took up a firing position in an alley parallel to the five-story Olympic Hotel. To the rear of the hotel, an enemy sniper moved behind a wall. Five stories above and to the left, another sniper moved on a veranda.

I realized we couldn't get a clear shot from where we were. I told a Delta sniper, "We're going to have to move on them."

We bumped up, moving forward to within less than 100 yards.

As we settled into our new position, the enemy had already begun firing into the target building where Delta assaulted. This felt like a setup to me. They were too well prepared. It seemed like too much of a coincidence that those snipers had set up so perfectly. *Probably a United Nations leak.*

The ground sniper sticking his rifle over the wall, approximately 100 to 150 yards away, aimed his scope at the Rangers in my convoy. The sniper had a good shooting position, only exposing his head. With a squeeze of my trigger, I overexposed his head.

From the fifth floor of the hotel, two enemy snipers fired into the target house, where the Delta assaulters were. This is an assaulter's worst nightmare. While the assaulter takes down the building and controls everything inside, suddenly bullets come through the windows at him from the outside.

From where I was, I couldn't get a clear shot.

I looked over at the Delta operator. "We need to move on these two or it's going to get real bad."

We slipped through the alley and took positions behind a pillar to our right. Still didn't have a good shot.

The two men on the fifth floor continued to pop out, spray at Delta's assault force, then pop back inside.

The Delta operator and I moved forward again. Finding a good spot, I lay in the prone position while my partner protected the perimeter around me. I set the red dot of my sight on the spot where the bad guy had appeared on the right. In sniper talk, it's called an ambush—aiming at a point and waiting for the target to appear there. The same technique could be used for a running target—aiming at a spot ahead of the runner's path. When the man with the AK-47 appeared on the right, I squeezed the trigger, hitting his upper torso. He popped back into the building and didn't pop out again. The second man made the same mistake.

At least thirty minutes had passed since we'd arrived. Every minute we stayed in the target area increased the level of danger. Over the radio came the command to return to the convoy. On my way through the alley, heading back to the cutvee, a ricochet hit me in the back of the left knee, knocking me to the dirt. For a moment, I couldn't move. On a fear scale of 1 to 10, 10 being out of my mind with fear, the needle jumped up between the 2 and the 3. The pain surprised me, because I had reached a point in my life when I really thought I was more than human. I was better trained. People around me got shot or injured, but not me. Even other SEALs got shot or injured because they were not me. *That's why you fell off that caving ladder—because you're not Howard Wasdin. That's why you couldn't pass me on the O-course—because you're not Howard Wasdin.* Even after getting shot that first time in the Battle of Mogadishu, I clung to my arrogance. I was stunned with disbelief more than anything else.

Dan Schilling, the CCT, appeared. Casanova arrived and calmly shot one booger-eater. Then another. A medic had just started treating me when Dan grabbed my bandolier and pulled me out of the enemy's kill zone. The medic stuffed my leg full of Kerlix gauze and wrapped it up. Then I was on my feet again.

The bad guys burned tires—a signal to their comrades to join the fight and a black smoke screen to obscure our vision. Militiamen with AK-47s popped up from behind smoke, side streets, and buildings—everywhere. As soon as I shot someone down, a replacement popped up. Unarmed women walked out as spotters, then pointed out our positions to the enemy. RPGs went off.

Aidid's men yelled into megaphones. I didn't understand that their words meant "Come out and defend your homes," but I understood they meant us harm.

One of the 5-ton trucks in our convoy smoldered from being

hit by an RPG. Someone in our convoy finished off the truck with a thermite grenade so it wouldn't fall into enemy hands. The vehicle flamed brightly.

Delta loaded two dozen flexicuffed prisoners into two of the remaining 5-ton trucks. Included among the prisoners was Aidid's top political adviser, Foreign Minister Omar Salad. Although Delta missed snatching Qeybdid, they'd captured a lieutenant of similar rank, Mohamed Assan Awale. They found a bonus, too, a clan chieftain named Abdi Yusef Herse.

At thirty-seven minutes, word came over the radio, "Super Six One down." An RPG had shot down a Black Hawk with a cartoon of Elvis Presley on its side, captioned VELVET ELVIS. Its pilot was Chief Warrant Officer Cliff Wolcott. Now our mission shifted from a prisoner snatch to a rescue.

We loaded up in the convoy to move out again. Aiming a rifle down an alley lay a Ranger who didn't look more than twelve years old.

I sat in the driver's seat calling to him, "Load up, let's go!"

The kid remained frozen.

I hopped out of the cutvee, ran over to the corner of the building, and kicked him.

He looked up at me with dazed eyes.

"Load your ass into the vehicle!"

He picked himself up and climbed into his Humvee.

Sometimes the young Rangers got so focused on the one thing they were supposed to do that they lost sight of the big picture. Their vision didn't widen in response to changes in the environment, and their ears missed verbal commands. Experiencing sensory overload of the sympathetic nervous system, they couldn't catch everything that was going on.

Fortunately, my father's harshness to me as a child had prepared me for difficulties like this. Adding to that preparation were Hell

Week, SEAL Team Two, SEAL Team Six, Marine Corps Scout Sniper School—intense training for years. The more you train in peace, the less you bleed in war. Desert Storm helped prepare me. I had developed a tolerance for sensory overload. Some of these Rangers had only been out of high school a couple of years.

Sourpuss wasn't with us. He was evacuating a Ranger casualty back to the compound. Riding in the main convoy, I drove out of the target area. With my left hand on the wheel, my right fired the CAR-15. AK-47 rounds came at us left and right. As bullets passed over my head, they created pressure waves faster than the speed of sound, waves that crashed into each other like two hands clapping. I heard the rounds coming—the clap—then the sound of them passing by.

White trails of smoke stretched out, resulting in exploding RPGs that shook the air, filling it with a bitter smell. The smell of burning tires and burning refuse rose above the normal stench of Mogadishu, stinking like hell.

Our .50 caliber machine gun rattled off, shaking our Humvee and pounding our ears. The .50 could chew through concrete, metal, flesh—it literally knocked out walls. Unfortunately, the enemy had .50s, too, bolted to the beds of their pickup trucks courtesy of Osman Atto's garage. The trucks ducked in and out of alleys shooting at us.

A helicopter gun blasted at the enemy, demolishing the side of a building. Somalis ran in all directions. Some screamed. Some froze. Dead people and a dead donkey lay on the ground.

Aidid's people are way better equipped than we thought, they fight better than we thought, and there are a lot more of them armed than we thought. Now I was afraid we were going to get our asses kicked. On my fear scale, the needle jumped past 3 and hit 5. Anyone who says he wasn't scared in combat is either an idiot or a liar. Everyone becomes scared. It's a healthy fear. I'd never want to go into combat with someone who wasn't a little afraid. What makes a warrior is being able to control and focus that fear. He develops this ability to control fear by believing he *can* control fear. This belief is gained by having overcome fear in previous experiences, seeing Teammates overcome such fears, knowing that he is an elite warrior, and channeling that anxious energy to boost his performance.

In our convoy, we had wounded men in *every* vehicle. We still wanted to rescue Velvet Elvis and his crew in the downed Super Six One. Nearing a road where a couple of Rangers lay wounded, I thought, *What the hell is wrong with these Somalis? We're here to stop the civil war, so people can get food, and they're killing us. This is how we're repaid?* I couldn't believe it. I pulled our cutvee off the road and stopped. The first Ranger I picked up was shot in the leg. We loaded him in the back of our cutvee. Then we loaded the other one, who'd been shot in the web of his hand—not such a debilitating injury. As I returned to the driver's seat, I looked back. The Ranger with the wounded leg was helping resupply us with ammo while the other Ranger sat there in a daze with his head down staring at his wounded hand.

The Ranger resupplying us with ammo was hit again, this time in the shoulder, but he kept feeding us ammo in the front. Then a round tore into his arm. He *still* kept feeding us ammo.

Meanwhile, the Ranger who'd been shot once through the web of his hand remained out of it, the needle on his fear meter stuck on 10. He was the only Ranger I saw back down from the fight. Then again, it's not every day a person gets shot. His reaction of shock is understandable—he was just a young kid in a horrific battle. All of the Rangers fought bravely.

Stepping hard on the accelerator, I caught up with the rest of the convoy. It turned right on a dirt road. When the first Humvee slowed down at the intersection, each vehicle behind was forced to slow down, creating an accordion effect. Then we turned right again, toward the south—but we had just come from the south.

I was getting pissed at our ground convoy leader, Lieutenant Colonel Danny McKnight, but I didn't know he was just doing what the birds in the sky told him. The Orion spy plane could see what was happening but couldn't speak directly to McKnight. So it relayed information to the commander at JOC. Next, the JOC commander called the command helicopter. Finally, the command helicopter radioed McKnight. By the time McKnight received directions to turn, he'd already passed the road.

All I knew was that I was getting shot at again, holes being poked into the holes of our cutvee. Our men in the back were getting hit. *Holy crap.* I wanted to stomp the accelerator to get out of the kill zone, but I could only go as fast as the Humvee in front of me. I shot militia coming at us from the side streets. Trying to drive and shoot militia ducking in and out of side streets, I'd be surprised if I had as much as a 30 percent kill rate.

People in buildings on the second floor shot down at us. I took some time to get into my ACOG scope, lining up the red dot on my first target and squeezing the trigger. One enemy down. Then another.

The bad guys had thrown up burning roadblocks and dug trenches to slow us down. While the convoy tried to drive through and around the roadblocks, the enemy ambushed us. Ahead and to the side of us, five women walked shoulder to shoulder holding their colorful robes out to both sides, advancing toward the convoy. When a Humvee reached the ladies' position, they pulled their dresses in and the men behind opened fire with their AK-47s on full auto. Later, they tried the same tactic on our cutvee. For the first time in the firefight, I flicked my selector switch to full auto. With one hand on the wheel, and the other holding my CAR-15, I fired thirty rounds, cutting down the women—and the four armed militia hiding behind them.

Then over the radio I heard that an RPG had taken down a Black Hawk piloted by Mike Durant. The word came down from the command helo to rescue Velvet Elvis first, then move on to Mike at the second crash site.

We stopped on the street, set up a perimeter, provided first aid, replenished ammo, and figured out what to do next. A medic bandaged the Ranger's shoulder and arm and other guys' wounds in our cutvee. Some Rangers looked like zombies, shock in their eyes.

A Delta operator came over. "I took a hit. Can you take a look at my shoulder?" A shot had clipped the hard armor plate in his back, but it didn't take him out of the fight.

The .50 cal machine gunner in another Humvee wore an armored vest, good for resisting small-caliber rounds. He had also inserted a specially designed 10"×12" ceramic plate in the front for protection against heavier rounds like the AK-47. However, he hadn't worn a plate on his back. Probably, like many other soldiers, he considered the extra plate in back too hot and too heavy. Besides, most shots are from the front anyway. He rolled the dice— and lost. Over the radio, we offered to let our .50 gunner replace him. The Humvee of the dead .50 gunner pulled up next to our vehicle. Inside, tears streamed down a Ranger's face as he held on to his buddy, one arm under his head. "You dumb sonofabitch. I told you. I told you to wear your back plate. I told you."

They pulled the dead gunner out, and our gunner replaced him. Without a qualified .50 gunner like our Ranger, their Humvee would've lost the ability to use its hardest-hitting weapon. Our gunner would end up saving their Humvee.

The convoy moved forward, and we turned left, heading east,

then left to the north. I didn't know that McKnight was hit, with shrapnel in his arm and neck. We stopped. McKnight radioed the command helo for directions, but miscommunication would send us on the wrong path again. The convoy continued north to Armed Forces Road and made a left.

I also didn't realize that Dan Schilling had taken over for McKnight while he was wounded. Dan succeeded in bypassing the convoluted communication loop and communicated straight to one of the helos. When Dan told them to vector us to the crash site, he assumed the helo knew we were headed to Velvet Elvis at the first crash site, but the helo assumed we were headed for the nearest one—Mike at the second crash site.

We turned left on Hawlwadig, heading near the Olympic Hotel and the target building. The convoy had gone around in a complete circle! We had showed our hand to Aidid's people during previous assaults, then launched the current assault during daylight, and now I was getting shot at again—I was beyond pissed! Experienced SEALs had taught us, "If you live through one ambush, go home, get in your rocking chair, and thank God the rest of your life." We'd driven back into a second. I remembered Commander Olson slapping me on the shoulder before we left the compound: "Shouldn't take long." *Yeah, right. These are the same booger-eaters who were shooting at us a while ago. What the hell is McKnight doing? Hey, dumb-ass, we just did this. It didn't work out too well the first time.*

While there was confusion on the radio about whether we were heading to the first crash site or the second, I heard that a crowd was closing in on Mike Durant with no ground forces in the area to help, and I remembered what happened to the Pakistanis when a crowd descended on them—they were hacked to pieces.

Our helicopter guns and rockets sent enemy bodies and body parts flying. When they paused, I called for even more fire. A pilot answered, "We're Winchestered." They had used up all their ammunition, including the 20 percent they were supposed to keep in reserve to defend themselves during the return to base. I was counting on that extra 20 percent. Even though they were out of ammo, the pilots buzzed over the bad guys almost low enough to hit them with the skids. The enemy turned away from us and directed their gunfire at the helos. While the booger-eaters aimed at the sky, we shot them. The pilots didn't just do that once. They did it at least six times that I remember. Our Task Force 160 pilots were badass, offering themselves up as live targets, saving our lives.

As I drove, I ran out of ammo in my CAR-15. I let it hang from the battle sling harnessed to me and drew the SIG SAUER 9 mm pistol from the holster on my right hip. Our convoy slowed down, and a booger-eater emerged in a doorway, aiming his AK-47 right at me. I brought my SIG SAUER across. Double tap. I'd made that double head shot over a thousand times in training. Under the present combat conditions, I rushed the shot. Miss. Adrenaline pumping at full blast, the world seemed to decelerate around me. The booger-eater pulled the trigger in slow motion. The bullet hit my right shinbone, practically blowing off my lower right leg. His bolt went back. The empty casing ejected. *This guy ain't playing around.* I took an extra half second and got on my front sight. Like John Shaw says, "Smooth is fast." Double tap. Both rounds hit him in the face. If I'd have taken that extra half second the first time, I could've capped his ass and saved my leg.

Our cutvee slowed down. *What the hell is wrong with our cutvee?* I tried to stomp on the accelerator and couldn't. Looking down on the floorboard, I saw a big toe pointing behind me. I didn't even realize it was my leg twisted inward. Surely I'd be in a lot more pain if it was my leg. I tried to step on the accelerator again. My right foot flopped. *Sonofabitch. That's my leg.* Reaching with my left foot, I jabbed the accelerator. *Wow, this is some really serious crap. I better get on top of my game.* Even though this was my second time getting shot during the battle, I still embraced my own superhuman strength. My fear meter rose to 6, but it hadn't reached 10. I felt numbness more than pain because my nerve receptors had overloaded. Although surprised for the second time during combat, I still felt superior as a SEAL Team Six sniper—Howard Wasdin.

I was furious with McKnight and called him on the radio. "Get us the hell out of here!"

Finally out of the danger zone, the convoy stopped to help the people who were leaking to stop leaking, feed our weapons more ammo, and plan our next move. Casanova helped me crawl over the center console and into the passenger seat, so he could drive.

My shattered bone had jagged edges that could slice into an artery and cause me to bleed to death. Casanova propped my wounded leg up on the hood of the Humvee and placed my left leg next to it as a brace. The elevation would also slow the blood flow. "I'm going to get you home," Casanova said.

The convoy moved out, and Casanova stepped on the gas. Our cutvee ran on three flat tires. The convoy made a U-turn and turned right at the Olympic Hotel, heading toward the first crash site, Velvet Elvis. It was like the movie *Groundhog Day,* repeating the same actions over and over again.

Five or ten minutes later, an enemy round shot through my left ankle. Unlike the fracture in my right shin, where my central nervous system shut off the pain, this one really hurt. My fear level rose from 6 to 7. My emotions toward the enemy rocketed off the anger scale. They had taken away my superhero powers. Suddenly, I realized I was in trouble.

True to form, our convoy missed Velvet Elvis at the first crash site—again. Then we stopped. Guys stepped out of their vehicles and set up a perimeter. McKnight got out of his vehicle with someone, and it looked like they laid a map on the hood of their Humvee, plotting our location. It was surreal. *While we're getting shot, why not walk into the 7-Eleven and ask for directions?*

Our convoy had failed twice to navigate its way to one of the downed pilots. We had used up most of our ammunition. Wounded and dead bodies filled our vehicles. Half of the men were severely wounded, including most of the leaders. If we didn't return to base and regroup, we might not have anyone left to launch a rescue.

Our cutvee had more holes in it than a sponge. The side mirrors dangled from their L-brackets. As the convoy moved forward again, our cutvee hit a land mine. The ballistic blankets covering the floor saved us from fragmentation. Casanova pulled off the road, where our cutvee died. The booger-eaters descended on us. *We're about to be overrun.*

I remembered the old 1960 movie *The Alamo,* starring John Wayne as Davy Crockett. It was one of my favorite movies, and Davy Crockett was my favorite person in the Alamo. *This must be how Davy Crockett felt before they killed him: outgunned, under-manned, without protection. Seeing his people get wiped out while the enemy continued to advance. This is it. Howard Wasdin checks out in Mogadishu, Somalia, on the afternoon of October 3, 1993. My one regret is I haven't told the people I love that I love them enough. During my time on earth, it's what I should've done more of.* The first two people who came to mind were my children, Blake and Rachel. I probably only told them I loved them about six times a year. Part of the problem was that, with frequent training deployments and real-world ops, I just wasn't around for a large part of their lives. Even though I was married, now I didn't think of my wife, Laura. My relationship with the SEAL Team had been more important than my marriage. I wanted to tell Blake and Rachel how much I loved them.

My fear meter peaked at 8. It never reached 10. When you hit a 10, you can't function anymore. You succumb to the mercy of events going on around you. I wasn't dead yet. Firing back with my SIG, I tried to keep six or seven of the booger-eaters from surrounding us. Physically, I couldn't shoot effectively enough to kill anyone at that point. I had used up two of Casanova's pistol magazines and was down to my last. Over the radio, I heard that the QRF were on their way to rescue us—four hours into the gunfight. Quick Reaction Force—*what is their definition of "quick"?*

Our vehicle still disabled on the side of the road, I looked up to see the QRF drive past our road. *Sonofabitch. We had a chance to get rescued and there they go. They are going to leave us here to die.* Then the QRF stopped and backed up with a deuce-and-a-half. *Thank God, at least they can see us.* When they reached the road beside us, the booger-eaters took flight. The QRF stopped.

Casanova and Little Big Man helped transfer the wounded over to their vehicles.

A Ranger struggled to coil up a fast rope that had been dropped from a helicopter during the insertion—just doing what he'd done on training ops many times. In sensory overload, soldiers rely heavily on muscle memory, fighting the way they trained.

Unable to walk, I stared at the Ranger in disbelief. "This is not a training operation!" I yelled. "Put the rope down, get your ass in the deuce-and-a-half, and let's get out of here!"

The Ranger continued trying to recover the rope, not conscious of the situation around him and not listening to verbal commands.

I pointed my SIG SAUER at him. "I won't kill you, but you will walk with a limp if you don't get your ass in that truck!"

The Ranger looked confused for a moment before dropping the fast rope. He hurried into a vehicle.

Finally, my guys loaded me into the deuce-and-a-half. "Be careful with him," Casanova said. "His right leg is barely hanging on."

We rode back to the compound unmolested by Aidid's forces. Arriving inside the gates, we met chaos: forty to fifty American bodies laid out all over the runway with medical personnel trying to get them through triage—figuring out the nonsurvivable from the survivable, the critical from the less critical—and attending to them accordingly. A Ranger opened a Humvee tailgate—blood flowed out like water.

Casanova and Dan Schilling carried me to the triage area.

Still in daylight, the medics stripped off all my clothes and treated me. They left me lying naked on that runway covered with bodies. Exposed.

Once again, death had just missed me. Like it missed when the enemy shot down the QRF helo, killing three men. Like it missed when Aidid's militia massed to attack us at Pasha. Like it missed when mortars bombed the CIA compound I had visited the day before. Like all the other misses. I thought maybe Casanova and I could've made a difference if we'd been riding in the QRF helicopter flight when the three men died. It hadn't occurred to me that maybe I could've been killed. It hadn't occurred to me that God was looking out for us. Now forty-eight years old and not as cocky, I wonder, *Would I have been able to get the enemy before he got me? Maybe people would've been coming to my memorial ceremony.*

Before the Battle of Mogadishu, the Clinton administration's support for our troops had sagged like a sack of turds. They had rejected or removed M-2 Bradley infantry fighting vehicles, M-1 Abrams tanks, and AC-130 Spectre gunships. The Clinton camp was more interested in maintaining political points than keeping some of America's finest troops alive.

During the Battle of Mogadishu, eighteen Americans were killed and eighty-four wounded. Also, one Malaysian died and seven were injured. Two Pakistanis and one Spaniard were wounded. In spite of only about 180 soldiers fighting against nearly 3,000 of

Aidid's militia and civilian fighters, we captured Omar Salad, Mohamed Hassan Awale, Abdi Yusef Herse, and others. Thousands of Aidid's clan members were killed, with thousands more wounded. They'd depleted much of their ammunition. A number of the chieftains evacuated in fear of America's inevitable counterattack. Some were ready to turn in Aidid to save themselves. We had broken Aidid's back, and we wanted to finish the job.

In spite of the gains, President Clinton saw our sacrifices as losses. Even though we could've finished the job of taking down Aidid and getting food to the people, Clinton turned tail and ran. He ordered all actions against Aidid stopped. Four months later, Clinton released Osman Atto, Omar Salad, Mohamed Hassan Awale, Abdi Yusef Herse, and the other prisoners. *What?*

We had spent so much time working with local Somalis to build their trust, to convince them that we would be with them in the long run. Many of these Somalis risked their lives to help us. Some endangered their families. Our former Somali guards at Pasha joined in the Battle of Mogadishu, loyal to the end. Only one of them survived. Other Somalis died on our side trying to stop Aidid. We left our Somali friends dangling in the breeze. I felt like our sacrifices had been in vain. *Why did they send us if they weren't willing to finish the job?* We shouldn't have become involved in Somalia's civil war—this was their problem, not ours— but once we committed, we should've finished what we started: a lesson we are required to keep relearning over and over again.

Somalia lost the assistance of the international community to bring peace and food to the country. Chaos and starvation spiked sharply. Aidid tried to downplay his losses, but he would never rule over a united Somalia. He died in 1996 during an internal battle against his evil genius, Osman Atto.

13.

From the Ashes

The sun had disappeared when medical personnel whisked me away to the field hospital. The thought sank in that I might lose my leg. I was scared. At the hospital, a nurse gave me a shot of morphine. It didn't take effect. Turned out I was in the 1 percent of people whose receptor for morphine doesn't make the pain go away. My pale body shook, and sweat poured out of me as I clenched my teeth, trying to will the pain not to consume me. *Calm your pulse down. Slow your breathing. Block the pain; will it away. I could do it as a kid; why isn't it working yet? I could do it as a kid; why can't I do it now?* Finally, a doctor who figured out the problem gave me a shot of a different painkiller. I was evacuated to Ramstein Air Base in Germany, a flight of about eight hours, where the U.S. military has a large hospital.

I argued with the nurse who tried to give me a sedative before my operation, because I was sure they were going to amputate my leg. The doctor said he'd save it, and he did. When I woke up, my leg was in a metal frame with pins going into my bone to keep everything in place. The surgeon had also taken skin grafts from my thigh to cover the wound.

Everything had been done so quickly, and the hospital had been so overwhelmed with casualties from the battle, that I still had blood in my hair and under my fingernails from the Ranger I had carried back to the Humvee. Uncle Earl, from my wife's family, happened to be in Germany visiting one of his companies. He heard where I was and came to visit. When he saw me, he stared for a moment and then went ballistic on the staff until they started to clean me up.

The next day, a Delta guy from across the hall who had an injured shoulder came and visited me. We talked about the battle. He said, "I didn't have a good appreciation for you guys since you weren't actually part of our team, but you guys kicked ass." He wheeled me over to see another patient, Brad, one of the Delta snipers. I saw Brad's amputated leg—sheared off when an RPG hit his helo. He shook my hand and we started to talk as if everything were normal.

"Hey, they were able to save your leg," Brad said.

"I was told that if it had been a quarter of an inch more, they would've had to amputate." *Brad is taking this way better than I am, and his leg is cut off. Here I am feeling sorry for myself. Angry at the world and God. Here he is with no leg and a positive attitude.*

Seeing Brad was good therapy for me. He was probably thinking he was lucky, too. Brad was a sniper on Black Hawk Super Six Two—Velvet Elvis. When they saw a downed helicopter with a pilot being threatened by a crowd, two of his teammates demanded to be let down to help. It was too dangerous to land, so they roped down. They fought off the crowd until their ammunition ran out. Then they were killed. The pilot was taken hostage. (He would later be released.) Brad's teammates, Gary Gordon and Randy Shughart, would posthumously receive the military's highest award, the Medal of Honor.

A week later I was back in the United States for rehabilitation. Shortly afterwards, I heard Delta would be having a memorial service for the men who died in the battle. The army sent a plane for me. At the base, I was reunited with the men from the other parts of the service I'd fought alongside in Mogadishu. After that experience, I was closer to them than to my SEAL Team Six Teammates who hadn't been with me in combat.

The air force would award Tim Wilkinson the military's second-highest honor, the Air Force Cross (equal to the Navy Cross for Navy, Marine Corps, and Coast Guard; Distinguished Service Cross for Army). Scotty would receive the Silver Star, the military's third-highest honor. Dan Schilling received its next-highest honor, the Bronze Star.

They wheeled me past a wall where the names of the fallen Delta Force guys were written. I saw six pairs of desert combat boots, six M-16 rifles with bayonets stuck downward in the base of the display, six bayonets on the rifle butts, and a picture for each of the six men: Dan Busch, Earl Fillmore, Randy Shughart, Gary Gordon, Tim "Griz" Martin, and Matt Rierson. I remembered Griz, a prankster who came up with new and exotic ways to blow stuff up.

During the memorial service in the auditorium, the chaplain led everyone in prayer for the fallen men. Wives wept. Dan Busch's parents looked devastated. Dan was only twenty-five years old—incredibly young to be a Delta sniper—from Portage, Wisconsin. Squared away. A devout Christian. I never heard him say a cuss word—rare in the special operations community. Of the little free time we had, I spent much of it with Dan Busch.

A sergeant read the Last Roll Call. Each man in the unit answered, "Here." Except for the fallen men. The honor guard fired three volleys. A bugler played taps.

In our profession we knew it was a possibility when we took the job. Still, looking at their parents, wives, and kids really hit me hard. *These guys are really gone. Dan is gone. How come I get to live and they don't? Dan Busch was a much better person and Christian than I was. Why is he dead, and I'm still here?* I felt guilty that I had survived.

After the memorial, when Scotty, Tim, and I were hanging

out, a Delta guy asked who I was. They didn't recognize me in my beard. I had been too weak to shave.

Scotty and Tim told him who I was.

"Aw, hell." The Delta operator went to the other Delta guys and said, "Hey, Wasdin is here!"

They swarmed me, took me to Delta's Charlie Squadron ready room, and gave me beers in both hands. We hung out, and they laughed when I told them about giving my medication to the Ranger at Landstuhl. Afterward Delta had a party, but I had a fever and didn't have enough power in my engine to join them. I went back to my hotel room early.

Only Defense Secretary Les Aspin attended the memorial service. For the most part, the Clinton administration seemed to hope the Battle of Mogadishu would just conveniently disappear and America would forget.

After flying out the next morning to Georgia, I showed up at the hospital for my regular visit. I had diarrhea. My fever had worsened—my whole body ached like it was on fire. I felt disoriented. I was literally dying. A medical team descended on me and rushed me into the back, gave me a shot in each butt cheek, and put an IV in each arm. They removed the bandages from my leg and started working on it. The doctor, who had gone home, returned in his civilian clothes. "Where have you been?" he asked. "We've been trying to contact your house, but you weren't there. The blood test results from your previous visit showed that you have a staph infection." The deadly staph infection had crawled deep inside me by way of the pins in my leg. This partly explains why I didn't feel up to attending the party with Delta after the memorial.

On the hospital bed, I floated up and looked down at myself lying there. *I'm dying. This staph infection sucks a lot worse than combat.*

The next day, the doctor was visibly upset with me. "If you're going to stay under my care, you've got to give us a way to stay in contact with you. If not, you need to go back to Virginia and let those navy doctors take care of you." He was scared. The doctor had done me a favor by letting me rehab in his army hospital—and I repaid him by almost dying on him.

"Yes, sir."

They kept me in the hospital a couple of days until I recovered.

Sitting at home in my wheelchair, I committed one of the Team's gravest sins—feeling sorry for myself. I slipped deep into depression. After waking in the morning, I had to perform my pin care, cleaning the skin around the four big pins sticking out of my leg. If I didn't, the infection would crawl down the pins and into my bone—causing another staph infection like the one that almost killed me. Then I'd bandage everything back up. The whole process took fifteen to twenty minutes. Twice a day. Doing the pin care by myself was tough. I asked my wife and brother-in-law to help, but they didn't have the stomach. It looked terrible—there's nothing normal about four pins screwed into a bone. My skin graft looked nasty, the meat visible.

The walls were closing in on me. I wasn't accustomed to being trapped indoors, and my depression was bearing down on me. I had to get out of the house, so I decided to do something simple and routine, but even something as mundane as grocery shopping turned out to be a bigger blow to my weakened self-esteem. One day, while slowly wheeling myself down the aisle in a Winn-Dixie supermarket in Jesup, Georgia, I started to realize how good it felt to be out of the house, contributing to the family by shopping. Some return to a normal life.

Then a woman stared at my leg, her face twisted like she'd eaten a lemon. I had cut the right leg of my sweatpants off above the knee to accommodate my external fixator. Although the skin-grafted area was bandaged, the pins were visible. "Why don't you stay at home?" she said. "Don't you realize how gross that is?"

I got my leg shot off serving her country. Our country. *Maybe this is how ordinary Americans see me. Are they fine with us going off to die for them but don't want to see us wounded?* I was feeling too sorry for myself to realize that she didn't know who I was or how I was wounded. At the time, when my spirit lay in the dirt, her words kicked me in the teeth. I desperately needed to bounce back, but I couldn't. Those words punted me deeper into depression.

At home, I wheeled around the house in my chair, eating and killing time watching TV. I couldn't take a shower or a bath because I couldn't get my screws wet. I had to wash my hair in the sink and take a washcloth bath.

Every other day I did rehabilitation at the hospital in Fort Stewart. They gave me hot whirlpool treatments for my left foot, to shake loose the dead flesh. It hurt like getting shot again. They gave me crutches. They put me on bars to help me walk. The pain was so intense that I couldn't stop tears from coming out of my eyes—I'd been still for too long before the rehabilitation. Then I had to have another surgery. Later I would have three more.

Out of the SEAL Team Six loop and with no Team guys around, I suffered the withdrawal symptoms of being cut off from the camaraderie. I was in culture shock, too. People around town could talk to me about their lives, but I couldn't talk to them about mine. Away from my Teammates, I felt forgotten, too. With no real-world missions, I had gone cold turkey from adrenaline. Now I couldn't even walk. In the SEAL culture, where it pays to be a winner, I was the biggest loser. I was angry at the world in general and at God in particular. *Why did this have to happen to me?*

In retrospect, I see that God was letting me know I was only human, and that being a SEAL was just a job. *Howard, you were too hardheaded to listen to Me after you were shot once. You didn't listen to Me after the second shot. Here, big boy, let Me give you your third bullet hole. Now, do I have your attention? You are not Superman. You are God's gift to special operations only for as long as I allow it to be. You are where you are because of Me. Not because of you. This is My way of getting your attention. Now that I've got it, let Me mold you further. You are not the finished product.* He humbled me and brought me back down to earth. Made me become a father to my children. At the time, no one could've convinced me of all that, but looking back, getting shot in the leg was the best thing that ever happened to me.

One day, a buddy of mine called me. On his ranch, he had a special hybrid of deer that he bred with American whitetail deer.

"Come over and let's hunt a little."

"Yes. Yes! Let me get out of this house! Anything!"

He picked me up in his pickup truck, took me out to the field, and set me down in my wheelchair on the ground. He pushed me nearly 30 yards through light underbrush, then stopped. He pointed to a spot about 150 yards away. "Over there is where the deer usually come out."

I was so happy—waiting there for nearly an hour and a half.

A huge buck came out. Sitting in my wheelchair, I brought my rifle to my shoulder, pulled the trigger, and the deer went down. Perfect shot. After laying my rifle on the ground, I wheeled my chair over to the animal. Pushing my wheelchair along a dirt road took me a while.

I parked my chair next to the deer. The beautiful buck looked up at me. It snorted, then laid its head back down. It made a last gasp, as if all the air had been sucked out of its lungs. Hearing it die, I thought, *I'd have been just as happy to come out and watch you, instead of taking your life. I've seen enough things die.*

I was still willing to kill someone to save myself or save another person—willing to kill in the line of duty—but I never hunted again.

The rehab people treated me like a celebrity. At that time, I was the only combat-wounded veteran in their hospital. Every time I went in, five or ten people would show up to talk to me.

After six or seven weeks, my niece brought me a device that slipped over the pins in my legs, creating a rubber seal, so I could shower. I stood on one leg in the shower and lathered up my hair. It felt like the best gift I'd ever received.

In early December, two months after the longest day in my life, my hometown of Screven, Georgia, threw me a hero's welcome as part of the Christmas parade, with yellow ribbons everywhere. A big sign in the restaurant covered the front window: WELCOME BACK HOWARD, THE HOMETOWN HERO. Nearly all nine hundred of the townspeople must've signed it. People from Wayne County came out to line the streets, see me, and wish me well. They had no idea about the physical pain, the mental anguish, the loss, or the dark hole of depression that tormented me—before they honored me that way. They had no idea how much their welcome meant to me, appreciating me as part of the community. I didn't feel like such a loser.

The Navy flew Casanova, Little Big Man, Sourpuss, Captain Olson, and me to the Pentagon to award us the Silver Star. In Mogadishu, Captain Olson left headquarters to participate in rescuing men still pinned down. At our award ceremony, video cameras rolled and still cameras flashed. My citation read:

The President of the United States takes pleasure in presenting the Silver Star medal to Hull Maintenance Technician First Class Howard E. Wasdin, United States Navy, for service set forth in the following citation: For conspicuous gallantry

*and intrepidity in action against a hostile force during oper-
ation UNOSOM II in Mogadishu, Somalia on 3 & 4 October 1993. Petty Officer Wasdin was the member of a security
team in support of an assault force that conducted an air
assault raid into an enemy compound and successfully ap-
prehended two key militia officials and twenty-two others.
Upon receiving enemy small arms fire from numerous alleys, Petty Officer Wasdin took up a firing position and returned fire. As he assaulted down the alley with members of
his unit, he was wounded in the calf. Upon receiving combat
field condition medical attention, he resumed his duties and
continued to suppress enemy fire. As his convoy exfiltrated
the area with detainees, his element came under withering
enemy fire. Petty Officer Wasdin, along with the security
team, stopped to suppress enemy fire which had pinned
down the Ranger blocking force. Although twice wounded,
he continued to pull security and engage a superior enemy
force from his vehicle. Later, while attempting to suppress
enemy fire, during an attempted link-up for evacuation of
the helicopter crash site, Petty Officer Wasdin was wounded
a third time. His gallant efforts inspired his team members
as well as the entire force. By his superb initiative, coura-
geous action, and complete dedication to duty, Petty Officer
Wasdin reflected great credit upon himself and upheld the
highest tradition of the United States Naval Force.*

Later, I also received a whack on the pee-pee for disobeying a
direct order and helping the teenaged Somali boy who'd stepped
on a land mine—my most successful op in Somalia.

After my recovery I returned to the Team, but there was a new
officer in charge and we didn't get along. Delta told me they'd
like to have me move to them. My new commanding officer told

me he'd be my worst nightmare if I requested a transfer. He must have thought it would make him look bad. He should've been a politician instead of a SEAL operator.

About the same time, my wife and I divorced. That caused a strain with my kids. Although I should've known that family ties are stronger than job ties, I'd sacrificed my family for the Teams.

Yet despite that sacrifice, I could never return to being 100 percent of the sniper I used to be.

My thinking became darker. One day, I held my SIG SAUER P-226 pistol in my hand. *How bad would it be if I took this P-226 and ended everything with one 9mm bullet? There are worse things than death.* I convinced myself that everyone would be better off. They could collect on my life insurance.

Blake was visiting me. "Dad."

That one word snapped me out of it. Ending my life would've been selfish. *If I don't have anything else to live for, at least I have my children.* I never had those dark thoughts again.

I walked on crutches before I was supposed to, used a cane before I was supposed to, walked unassisted before I was supposed to, and started swimming before I was supposed to. Although people thought I would never walk without a limp, I did. Even though many thought I'd never run again, I did. After returning to the Team, I hit the gym every morning and did PT with them. I couldn't always keep up, but I consistently worked hard at it.

Although still experiencing daily pain and sleepless nights from my injuries, I recovered to the point that I could receive an assignment to protect Ambassador to the Philippines John Negroponte, who had received death threats.

After that, I returned to the Team. We did our routine workups: running, kill house, shooting range. I realized, *This isn't going to work out.*

I spoke to Six's command master chief. "I'm going to pack my stuff and head to Georgia. I'm in constant pain. My leg throbs all day. A lot of hip pain. Neck pain. I can't sleep too well."

At the time, I didn't know what was wrong with me. Having adjusted for my gunshot wound by changing my gait, I was carrying myself wrong—my externally rotated foot was affecting my hip. My neck compensated by going the other way. Sort of like a house: If the basement tilts to the right and sinks a little, the roof follows—except the neck pulls the opposite way.

"I understand exactly where you're coming from. If you want, I'll transfer you to any Team you want, send you to BUD/S to be an instructor . . . You can pick a division here: air ops, boat ops, demo . . . Whatever you want to do. Just tell me and it's yours."

I'd never be able to do what my Teammates were doing. I knew when I was at the top of my game. Now I was not. It was a harsh reality to face. *I'm not as good, not as fast, and my senses are not as keen as they used to be. Definitely not physically doing what I used to do.* "Thank you, Master Chief. But if I'm not going to be one of the Team guys doing the job, I'd rather just get on with the next phase of my life. Do something different. See what's out there."

Most of my adult life, I had been in the military. It would be a new adventure: *What can I do in the civilian world?*

14.

Fish out of Water

I struggled for a long time, trying to do things that were close to what I'd done in the navy. I trained security teams for the 1996 Summer Olympics in Atlanta, the Special Operations and Response Teams for the Federal Bureau of Prisons, and others like them. But between assignments, I struggled financially.

Hoping for more stability, I became a police officer just north of Miami in Hallandale Beach, Florida. I wanted to be like the ones who treated me well as a kid. Unfortunately, I came across a lot of kids who needed the same kind of help I'd needed, but little room in the daily work of being a city police officer for the kindness I'd been shown. Also, as a single father, I realized I couldn't make it financially as a police officer.

When a leading body armor company, Point Blank, offered me a job, I left law enforcement. Blake and I moved to Tennessee, and he fit in well at his new school. Life was good. The downside was that I often had to travel, so Blake had to stay with friends. Also, I felt it was important for us to live be closer to my daughter, who was back in Georgia. That meant another career change. Suddenly I found myself selling cars. Very successfully. It wasn't what I'd expected, but it was working out. At least I thought so. Turns out I'd lost track of what mattered.

On a Saturday afternoon in 2002, I had big plans to watch a video with Blake when my cousin Edward called, begging me to come out to dinner with him and his wife and a friend, Debbie. Long story short: Debbie and I were married a year later.

Among the other things Debbie brought into my life, she made me realize that I'd been walking through work. Car sales wasn't fulfilling—even though the good people of Wayne County bought from me, showing their love and appreciation for my military service. I began to think about some of the security consulting jobs that old military friends kept mentioning to me.

There was one other thing that interested me, but I kept talking myself out of it. Back when I was a police officer, I'd caught a kid—a good kid as it turned out—after a long foot chase. My body paid a big price for the chase for weeks afterward. My neck and lower back were killing me. A police officer from North Miami Beach had been recommending over and over that I visit a chiropractor, but I'd blown her off. After the chase, I was desperate. I remembered that the ambassador in the Philippines had also sworn by the help he got from his chiropractor.

Finally I went. The chiropractor evaluated me and found how my gunshot wound had led me to throw my body out of balance. After three treatments, I slept all the way through the night for the first time in years, nearly pain free. Just by visiting the chiropractor twice a month. *Wow!* After all the neurologists, orthopedic surgeons, and other doctors, a chiropractor gave me back my quality of life.

At that point, I thought chiropractors were like massage therapists or something like that. I had no idea that they studied to become doctors. *There really is something to this chiropractor thing.*

So in the back of my mind, while I was selling cars and looking into security consulting, I was also thinking about becoming a chiropractor. I'd even learned that the Department of Veterans Affairs would pay for the courses. But whenever Debbie and I talked about it, I came up with all kinds of reasons I shouldn't do it. "I won't be able to work full-time and go to school full-time. We'll have to tighten our budget. It's going to take a long time. I'll have to live near school until I graduate. A lot of driving back and forth . . ."

Debbie threw the BS flag. "You can go the rest of your life being miserable—never feeling fulfilled, never finding a job you really like again—or you can just do this. The sooner you get started, the sooner you'll be done, and you'll be happy with your occupation again. If you don't, you'll look back after four years and say, 'If I'd gone to school, I'd be finished by now.'" I married the right woman. In January 2005, at Life University in Marietta, Georgia, I started school to become a chiropractor.

15.

Healing

During my last year at school, my father had an abdominal aortic aneurysm. His abdominal aorta was blowing up like a balloon. Right before my final exams, he passed away. I found out I wasn't as tough as I thought I was.

After I had become a SEAL, I didn't worry about Dad kicking the crap out of me anymore. Our relationship had improved. After Somalia, I told him I loved him for the first time—then I told him every time I saw him after that. We hugged. The passage of time had mellowed him, too. During a family reunion shortly before his death, he told me how he approved of my new wife, Debbie. "She's a keeper. Don't mess up." He loved her. Regarding my new profession, he said, "When you open up your clinic, I'll be one of your first patients." Coming from a man who wouldn't go to a doctor unless he was dying, which was part of his undoing, his confidence in my future skills as a chiropractor meant a lot to me. I had received the acceptance, respect, and approval from my father that I'd always longed for.

My mother told me that later in life Dad was disappointed that he and I didn't have a better relationship. I didn't have the heart to tell her that when I was home, he had always been a dictator. He didn't have conversations with me—didn't build a relationship. I didn't cry as much about his death as I had about Uncle Carroll's.

Still, my dad raised me the only way he knew how, and I was sad when he died.

One day, about nine months later, Blake asked out of the blue, "Would you like to meet him?"

"Meet who?" I asked.

"Your real dad."

My biological father could have walked past me in the grocery store, and I wouldn't have known who he was. "Yeah, Blake. You know, I think I would."

We did a people search and found him. Then I made the phone call. At Christmas, I went to see Ben Wilbanks, my biological father. Ben said that my mother had taken us kids and run off to Georgia with Leon. In my mind, Ben's story kind of explains the quick move from Florida to Georgia and the quick adoption. I'm inclined to believe him, due to conflicting stories I got from my mother and sisters. Ben said he had spent years looking for me and could never find me. He turned out to be one of the nicest and most loving men I'd ever met. When he hugged me, I knew that I was really being hugged. Seeing Ben Wilbanks seemed to explain where I got my affectionate side—my capability for compassion and emotion. Ben had served in the army as a military policeman and worked most of his career as a truck driver, which is what he still does.

Blake and I continue to maintain a relationship with my biological father, Blake's grandfather. Whatever happened between my mother and Ben, she still hasn't forgiven him. Nor forgotten. For my part, I refuse to hold decisions made in their youth against either of them, because I wouldn't want to be held in contempt for all the decisions made by me in my youth.

I graduated with honors as a doctor of chiropractic in 2009. When I first started seeing patients is when I knew I'd made the right decision. They trust me, I figure out what's wrong with them, I help them feel better, and they love me for it. From the day I opened the doors of my clinic, Absolute Precision Chiropractic, I have been blessed with busy days treating members of the local and surrounding communities.

One of my patients, a thirteen-year-old boy, had been suffering from chronic headaches for four years. It turned out he experienced a bad car accident when he was little and lost the curve in his neck. He went from nearly twelve headaches a month on frequent medication to one or two headaches in the first ten weeks I saw him.

Another affirmation for me occurred when I treated a young lady who had brachial palsy. Her arm hadn't formed correctly, and she had a lot of nerve damage—she was barely able to move her right arm. I had been helping her with electrical stimulation, adjusting her, and administering other chiropractic techniques. She laterally moved her arm 42 degrees for the first time in her life. Then she flexed her arm forward toward me 45 degrees for the first time. My assistant cried. The fifteen-year-old girl cried from her exertion and success. Her father cried. I stepped out of the room—and cried. Helping patients like her helps lessen the guilt that still makes me wonder why I'm still alive when better men than me like Dan Busch are not.

Success stories like this let me know I made the right decision. I understand better why God spared me—he really did have a purpose for me after my life as a SEAL. I truly feel that this is the path God intended for me when he spared my life in Somalia.

Even though Blake is in his twenties now, whenever he visits, I give him a good-night hug. I give the same affection to my step-daughter, Eryn, whom I consider my own daughter. I give my wife, Debbie, a hug or a kiss every time I leave or return to the house.

Years ago I had questioned why my life had been spared. To-day I am thankful that God spared my life and equally thankful for the path that was laid before me. I once again have a positive mind, body, and spirit. Professionally and personally, life is good again.

SPECIAL OPERATIONS
WARRIOR FOUNDATION

The Warrior Foundation's mission is to provide a college education to every child who has lost a parent serving in the U.S. Special Operations Command and its units. The Warrior Foundation also provides immediate financial help to special operations personnel severely wounded in the war against terrorism.

It was founded in 1980 to provide college educations for the seventeen children surviving the nine special operations men killed or incapacitated during the failed attempt to rescue American hostages from the U.S. Embassy in Tehran. It was named the Colonel Arthur D. "Bull" Simons Scholarship Fund, in honor of a legendary Army Green Beret who repeatedly risked his life on rescue missions. It later merged with similar funds, expanding its scope.

Today, the Warrior Foundation is committed to providing scholarship grants, *not loans,* to more than seven hundred children. These children survive more than six hundred special operations personnel, from all branches of the military, who gave their lives in patriotic service to their country.

To date, 121 children of fallen special operations warriors have graduated from college.

Contact information:
Special Operations Warrior Foundation
P.O. Box 13483

Tampa, FL 33690
www.specialops.org
E-mail: warrior@specialops.org
Toll-free phone: 1-877-337-7693

HOWARD'S ACKNOWLEDGMENTS

I'd like to thank my Lord and Savior Jesus Christ for all my blessings. Thanks for the guardian angels that kept me alive while in harm's way.

I'm very thankful for the people of Wayne County, Georgia, who have always stood behind me and been a source of strength, motivation, and inspiration.

Special thanks to my patients, who have allowed me to be their chiropractor. I love you all.

Thanks to my coauthor, Steve Templin, who resurrected a dead project in this book and worked tirelessly to perfect it.

I'm truly blessed to have been given two careers that were/are exceptional and that I truly love. I'm happy every day to come to work and help people, which, as corny as it sounds, was the reason I became a SEAL in the first place.

God bless America and our fighting men and women.

STEVE'S ACKNOWLEDGMENTS

I've been blessed. During Basic Underwater Demolition/SEAL Training Indoctrination with Class 143, I first met Howard Wasdin. We'd finished another brutal day of training, and Howard asked, "Who wants to go with me for a jog on the beach?" I thought he was nuts. *Hadn't we had enough for the day?!* And even nuttier were the guys who followed him. Howard and I became friends—we hung out with the guys in Tijuana on Saturday, and he dragged me to church on Sunday. Our paths split when I injured myself and rolled back to Class 144, but I never forgot him.

Years later, waiting for a flight at the Los Angeles International Airport, I slipped into the bookstore to kill some time and soon found myself in the middle of a war zone—I had picked Mark Bowden's excellent book *Black Hawk Down*. I looked in the index to see if any SEALs were involved. To my surprise, I ran across Howard's name. *No way*. I thought for sure somebody would write the rest of his story, and I'd be one of the first to buy it. But years went by and no book. Thanks to Facebook, I hooked up with Howard again. I'm fortunate he waited to tell his story—coauthoring his biography has been the ride of a lifetime—thanks, Howard!

I'm also blessed that my wife, Reiko, and children, Kent and Maria, have given me a taste of heaven. Of course, I couldn't have come into this world without my mother, Gwen, who has always been there to support me and let me do my own thing—some of my fondest early memories are exploring the Arizona desert alone before I was old enough to attend school. I'm thankful to my father, Art, for the times he was there for me. My grandfather, Robert, taught me how to negotiate 10 percent off a can of paint at the hardware store. Grandpa loved me like a son, and I loved him like a father. I'm sure he's looking down on this book with a smile—writing has been my dream since early elementary school. Carol Scarr gave Howard and me excellent writing advice on earlier drafts and has been a great friend. Others also gave helpful comments.

It would be difficult to write and research without the support of Meio University, where I am currently an associate professor. Scott Miller, Trident Media Group, showed Howard and me all the professionalism an agent can show and more—reading our manuscript during his Easter vacation; when he returned to work, found us our first publisher within twenty-four hours. Marc Resnick, St. Martin's Press, outshined the others to seal the deal and has maintained his enthusiasm, making this process a joy.

I'm deeply honored that General Henry Hugh Shelton (Retired) took time from his busy schedule to give support. Also, the Delta Force major who wrote *Kill Bin Laden,* Dalton Fury, offered his help early on, for which I'm grateful. Thanks to Randy "Kemo" Clendening (former SEAL Team Two operator) for assistance, too.

I'd like to thank Debbie Wasdin for her friendship and help. Eryn Wasdin chauffeured me and made me smile.

While I worked with Howard to finish up the book, Tammie Willis, a licensed medical massage therapist at Absolute Precision, gave me the best massage I've ever had—you're awesome, Tammie. The rest of the Absolute Precision staff was wonderful, too: Miki, Kelly, and everyone.

Thank you to the people of Wayne County, Georgia, who made me feel at home during my stay.

GLOSSARY

AC-130 Spectre: It superseded the Vietnam-era AC-47 gunship a.k.a. "Spooky" or "Puff the Magic Dragon." The spectre is an Air Force plane capable of spending long periods of time in the air, sometimes carrying two 20 mm M-61 Vulcan cannons, one 40 mm L/60 Bofors cannon, and a 105 mm M-102 howitzer. Sophisticated sensors and radar help it detect enemy on the ground.

AK-47: The name is a contraction of Russian: *Avtomat Kalishinikova obraztsa 1947 goda* (Kalishnikov's automatic rifle model of year 1947). This assault rifle fires a .308 (7.62×39 mm) round up to an effective range of 330 yards (300 meters) and holds 30 rounds. It was developed in the Soviet Union by Mikhail Kalashnikov in two versions: the fixed-stock AK-47 and the AKS-47 (S: *Skladnoy priklad*) variant equipped with an underfolding metal shoulder stock.

AT4: 84mm, one-shot light anti-tank rocket.

Agency: Central Intelligence Agency (CIA). Also known as "Christians in Action."

Asset: Local personnel providing intelligence.

BDU: Battle Dress Uniform.

Blowout kit: Medical pouch.

Booger-eater: Generic term for *bad guy*.

BUD/S: Basic Underwater Demolition/SEAL training.

CAR-15: Colt Automatic Rifle-15. One of the family of AR-15 (Arma-Lite Rifle) and M-16 rifle-based small arms. Later versions of the AR-15/M-16 assault rifles were short-barreled. Typically 11.5 inches for a Cold Commando (Model 733), a 14.5 in. barrel for the M-4 Carbine, and a 20 in. barrel for an M-16. The CAR-15 is an earlier version of the M-4 assault rifle with a retractable telescopic buttstock, firing .223 (5.56 mm) rounds, and holding 30 rounds in the magazine. Colt wanted identification of the CAR-15 with its other products, but the CAR designation eventually wound up as a law-enforcement weapon and the M-16 as a military small arm.

CCT: Combat Control Team/combat controllers. Air Force special operation pathfinders who can parachute into an area and provide reconnaissance, air traffic control, fire support, and command, control, and communications on the ground—particularly helpful in calling down death from above.

CO: Commanding officer.

CQC: Close quarters combat.

CVIC: Aircraft Carrier Intelligence Center. The first *C* actually stands for "cruiser." The *V* comes from the French word *voler*, meaning "to fly." Used together, *CV* is the navy hull classification symbol for "aircraft carrier."

Cadre: Instructors. Sometimes means leaders.

Cammy, cammies: Camouflage.

Caving ladder: Portable wire ladders for climbing.

Chemlights: Glow sticks. Light sticks containing chemicals activated by bending.

Correct Dope: Adjust the scope to adjust for windage and distance.

Cutvee: A cut down Humvee without a top, doors, or windows; a.k.a. M-998 cargo/troop carrier.

Dam Neck: Dam Neck, Virginia, home of SEAL Team Six.

Delta: Delta Force. The army's tier-one unit tasked with conducting counterterrorism and counterinsurgency.

Deuce—and-a-half: A truck that carries 2.5 tons.

Dope: Knowledge, intelligence, poop (Navy Slang). *Also see* Correct Dope.

E & E: Escape and Evasion. Getting out of Dodge.

Exfil: Exfiltrate.

External fixator: A device used in treating fractures. A surgeon drills holes into the uninjured part of the bone near the fracture, then screws pins into the bone. Outside the limb, a metal rod attaches to the pins to hold them in place. The pins and rod make up the external fixator. A.k.a. "halo."

Fantail: A ship's stern overhang.

Fast-rope: Kick a thick rope out of the door. Then, wearing special gloves to prevent burning the hands, grab the rope with hands and feet while sliding down.

FFP: Final Firing Position; a sniper's hide, i.e., the camouflaged pit or tree blind from where a sniper fires.

Fireflies: Handheld infrared strobe lights.

Flashbang: Stun grenade using a nonlethal flash of bright light and loud blast to disorient enemies.

Full package: In Mogadishu, this was at least a hundred men, including a Humvee blocking force, Little Birds with Delta snipers, and Black Hawks with Rangers and Delta operators.

HAHO: High Altitude High Opening; a parachute jump by personnel at 25,000 to 35,000 feet wherein the parachute is opened quickly (while high in the air).

HALO: High Altitude Low Opening; a parachute drop made delivering supplies, equipment, or personnel by freefalling until the dropped objects are low enough to open the chute and safely land on target.

Helo: Helicopter

HUMINT: Human intelligence. Intelligence gained and provided by human sources: agents, couriers, journalists, prisoners, diplomats, NGOs, refugees, etc.

IED: Improvised Explosive Device. A homemade explosive device used in unconventional (illegal) warfare.

JOC: Joint Operations Center.

JSOC: Joint Special Operations Command, located at Pope Air Force Base and Fort Bragg in North Carolina. JSOC commands Special Mission Units which include SEAL Team Six, Delta, and the air force's 24th Special Tactics Squadron.

KIM: Keep In Mind; memorization games for scout-snipers.

Khat: A flowering plant native to Somalia, which contains a stimulant that causes excitement, loss of appetite, and euphoria (a.k.a. African "speed").

KN-250: Night-vision rifle scope. Night vision amplifies available light from sources like the moon and stars, converting images into green and light green instead of black and white. The result lacks depth and contrast but enables the sniper to see at night.

Knot: One knot equals roughly 1.15 miles per hour.

Little Bird: Special operations light helicopters. The MH-6 and AH-6 (attack variant) were both used in Mogadishu. Armament includes guns, rockets, and missiles.

LST: Lightweight Satellite Terminal; an encrypted radio that can send burst packets to a satellite for fast relay.

MRE: Meal, Ready-to-Eat. Field ration in lightweight packaging. Sometimes referred to as "Meal, Refusing-to-Exit" because the low dietary fiber content can cause constipation.

Macawi: A colorful Somali kiltlike garment.

NOD: Night Optical Device.

OP: Observation post.

Op: Operation.

P-3 Orion: Navy spy plane.

PJ: Air Force pararescue special operations unit focused on rescuing pilots downed in enemy territory and providing emergency medical treatment.

PLO: Palestine Liberation Organization. A political, paramilitary, and terrorist organization recognized by a hundred states as representative of the Palestinians.

PT: Physical Training.

Pasha: Codename for our safe house in Mogadishu.

QRF: Quick Reaction Force made up of the Army's 10th Mountain Division, 101st Aviation Regiment, and 25th Aviation Regiment.

Rangers: A rapid light infantry unit that can fight against conventional and special operations targets. The Army Rangers in Mogadishu came from Bravo Company, 3rd Ranger Battalion.

RPG: Rocket-propelled grenade.

SAS: Special Air Service, Britain's tier-one special operations commando unit. Australia and New Zealand derived their SAS from this British unit.

SEALs: The U.S. Navy's elite Sea, Air, and Land commandos.

SERE: Survival, Evasion, Resistance, and Escape.

SIG Sauer P-226 Navy 9 mm: Schweizerische Industrie Gesellschaft—German for "Swiss Industrial Company." Pistol with phosphate corrosion-resistant finish on the internal parts, contrast sights, and an anchor engraved on the slide. Holds fifteen rounds in the magazine. Designed especially for the SEALs.

SIGINT: Signals Intelligence. Intelligence gathered by intercepting signals between people (communications intelligence) and electronic signals (electronic intelligence) not directly involved in communication such as radar. Also the people responsible for gathering such intelligence.

Staph infection: *"Staph"* is short for *"staphylococcal,"* a strain of bacteria that produces toxins similar to those in food poisoning, which can kill.

Task Force 160: Nicknamed the "Night Stalkers," this army helicopter unit usually operates at night, flying fast and low, to avoid radar detection.

Thermite grenade: Grenade containing thermite, a chemical that burns at approximately 4,000 degrees Fahrenheit/2,200 degrees Celsius.

UDT: Underwater Demolition Team. The frogmen, ancestors of SEALs.

UNOSOM: United Nations Operation in Somalia.

Unit: U.S. Army Delta Force.

VC: Vietcong. Guerrilla and regular Communist units that fought the South Vietnamese and America during the Vietnam War.

Win Mag: Winchester Magnum. The .300 Win Mag holds four rounds of .300 ammunition. Usually used with a Leupold 10-power scope. For evening, a KN-250 night vision scope slides over the top of the Leupold.

REFERENCES

Boesch, R. & Dockery, K. (1995). In B. Fawcett (Ed.), *Hunters & Shooters* (pp. 1-32). New York: Avon.

Bosiljevac, T. L. (1990). *SEALs: UDT/SEAL Operations in Vietnam*. Boulder, Colorado: Paladin Press.

Bowden, M. (2001). *Black Hawk Down*. New York: Signet.

Carney, J. T., & Schemmer, B. F. (2002). *No Room for Error: The Covert Operations of America's Special Tactics Units from Iran to Afghanistan*. New York: Random House Publishing Group.

Chalker, D., & Dockery, K. (2002). *One Perfect Op: An Insider's Account of the Navy SEAL Special Warfare Teams*. New York: HarperCollins.

Couch, D. (2001). *The Warrior Elite: The Forging of SEAL Class 228*. New York: Three Rivers Press.

Coulson, D. O., & Shannon, E. (1999). *No Heroes: Inside the FBI's Secret Counter-Terror Force*. New York: Pocket Books.

Eversmann, M., & Schilling, D. (2006). *The Battle of Mogadishu: Firsthand Accounts from the Men of Task Force Ranger*. New York: Presidio Press.

Gormly, R. A. (1998). *Combat Swimmer: Memoirs of a Navy SEAL*. New York: Penguin Group.

Lechner, J. O. (1994). *Combat Operations in Mogadishu, Somalia Conducted by Task Force Ranger*. Fort Benning, Georgia: United States Army Infantry School.

References

Loeb, V. (February, 2000). The CIA in Somalia. *The Washington Post*.

Loeb, V. (April, 2001). Confessions of a Hero. *The Washington Post*.

Marcinko, R., & Weisman, R. (1992). *Rogue Warrior*. New York: Pocket Books.

Maren, M. (2010). *Somaliarchive: The Mysterious Death of Ilaria Alpi*. www.netnomad.com.

Murphy II, K. M. (1994). *Multi-National Combined Arms Breaching (MOUT) in Somalia*. Fort Benning, Georgia: United States Army Infantry School.

Norris, T. (2009). *Medal of Honor Series: Thomas Norris*. Pritzker Military Library.

Norris, T., & Thornton, M. (2006). *Medal of Honor Series: Thomas Norris and Michael Thornton*. Pritzker Military Library.

Pfarrer, C. (2004). *Warrior Soul: The Memoir of a Navy SEAL*. New York: Random House Publishing Group.

Rysewyk, L. A. (May, 1994). *Infantry Officers' Advanced Course*. Fort Benning, Georgia: United States Army Infantry School.

Stubblefield, G. & Halberstadt, H. (1995). *Inside the U.S. Navy SEALs*. Osceola, Wisconsin: MBI Publishing Company.

Walsh, M. J., & Walker, G. (1994). *SEAL!* New York: Pocket Books.